Frank

Frank Gehry On Line

Esther da Costa Meyer

Princeton University Art Museum

Yale University Press
New Haven and London

Frank Gehry: On Line is published by the Princeton University Art Museum, Princeton, New Jersey 08544-1018, and distributed by Yale University Press, P.O. Box 209040, New Haven, Connecticut 06520-9040.

The publication has been supported with funds from the Publications Committee of the Department of Art and Archaeology, Princeton University, The Andrew W. Mellon Foundation, the Mildred Clarke Pressinger von Kienbusch Memorial Fund, and the Joseph L. Shulman Foundation Fund for Publications.

The book was published on the occasion of the exhibition *Frank Gehry: On Line*, on view at the Princeton University Art Museum from October 4, 2008, through January 4, 2009.

Managing Editor: Jill Guthrie
Assistant Editor: Sarah Noreika
Copy Editor: Brian Bendlin
Designer: CoDe. New York Inc., Jenny 8 del Corte Hirschfeld, Franck Doussot, and Mischa Leiner
Printer: Meridian Printing, East Greenwich, Rhode Island
Slipcase: Sea Group Graphics, Thorofare, New Jersey

Library of Congress Control Number: 2008924255
ISBN: 978-0-300-12214-5

The book was typeset in Berthold Akzidenz Grotesk Buch and Berthold Akzidenz Grotesk Buch Rounded, and printed on Scheufelen PhoeniXmotion Xenon.

Printed and bound in the United States of America

Contents

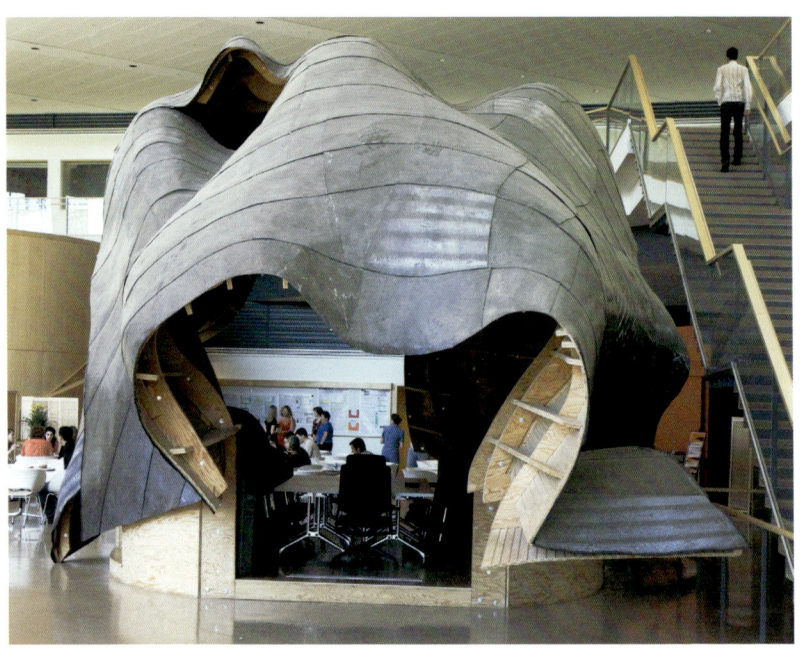

Frontispiece. Horse's Head Sculpture, Carl Icahn Laboratory, Princeton University, Princeton, New Jersey, 1999

Preface and Acknowledgments

The completion of Princeton's Peter B. Lewis Science Library is an occasion for special celebration. Frank Gehry has distinguished himself internationally by challenging the parameters of architecture even within the avant-garde. It is therefore only fitting that Princeton University, which prides itself on its position at the forefront of scientific research, should commission Gehry Partners to design a building so central to the university's research mission. Strictly speaking, this is not the first work by Gehry to be built on campus. Inside the Carl Icahn Laboratory, Gehry designed a witty and unconventional conference room, a building-within-a-building shaped like a horse's head, which can be used for small seminars (see frontispiece). In fact, Gehry's two structures are on opposite sides of the same thoroughfare, the main road of access into Princeton and the university.

To honor the inauguration of the new building, the Princeton University Art Museum has organized an exhibition of Gehry's drawings and published a small book on the subject. Because works on paper are fragile and extremely sensitive to light, these drawings are rarely shown in public. It is therefore all the more gratifying to have the opportunity to present them at the art museum, a most appropriate venue given the institution's commitment to supporting projects on contemporary architecture and design.

Architectural drawings are the first step in a long and complex process that culminates in the finished building. This is particularly striking in the case of Gehry, for whom the sketch is a cognitive tool, a way of transcribing thoughts and of seeking solutions to technical and aesthetic problems. With their spontaneity and work-in-progress informality, Gehry's drawings record the intellectually driven exploration that fuels architectural investigation. As such, they serve as an apt metaphor for the spirit of inquiry and relentless pursuit of ideas that is at the core of the university's mandate.

Almost all the sketches on display, some of which have never been published, were executed over the last two decades. They represent an array of international projects, both built and unbuilt, ranging from the United States and Canada, to Germany, Spain, Great Britain, and Israel, and from museums and concert halls to university buildings and private residences. Large architectural commissions develop slowly over time so that different projects often overlap, and the corresponding sketches can extend over lengthy periods. In presenting these works, the museum has thus avoided a strict chronological approach, and focused instead on what all the projects have in common: the quest for form out of the swirling chaos and turbulence of creativity.

Many people were instrumental in helping bring this project to fruition. Quite aside from his generosity in lending us his drawings and models, Frank Gehry's willingness to share insights into his work were invaluable to the completion of this exhibition and its catalogue essay. Equally important was the contribution of Craig Webb, the project designer for the Science Library, who kindly offered assistance throughout the different phases of preparation. Several members of Gehry Partners worked hard to secure the necessary documentation. We have benefited greatly from Keith Mendenhall's expert advice in the early days of the project. For the last two years, Laura Stella has helped us choose drawings, photographs, and models, and greatly facilitated every step of the long period of preparation that inevitably precedes any exhibition. Rhiannon Gharibeh was a most effective liaison with Craig Webb's team and helped solve the more intricate technical problems.

At every step along the way, Robert Barnett, the university's program manager for the arts, and Henry Thomas, senior project manager, design and construction, assisted us in solving unforeseen problems at the university level. The book was generously supported by the Department of Art and Archaeology and its publications fund, The Andrew W. Mellon Foundation, the Mildred Clarke Pressinger von Kienbusch Memorial Fund, and the Joseph L. Shulman Foundation Fund for Publications.

To Jenny 8 del Corte Hirschfeld and Mischa Leiner of CoDe. New York Inc., we owe the design of the catalogue with its ingenious slipcase, and of the exhibition itself. Jill Guthrie, the art museum's managing editor, steered the book through to completion with extraordinary skill, endless patience, and infectious good humor. Her assistant, Sarah Noreika, provided excellent assistance with bibliography and photographs. Meridian Printing under the guidance of Daniel Frank is to be thanked for the outstanding quality of the printing.

The museum and its personnel could not have been more eager to help. I am grateful especially to Acting Director Rebecca Sender; Michael Brew, business manager; Caroline Harris, curator of education and academic programs; Michael Jacobs, senior preparator; Gerritt Meaker, preparator; Calvin Brown, assistant curator of prints and drawings; and Alexia Hughes, associate registrar. I extend my thanks, as well, to Elizabeth Saluk, rights and reproductions coordinator at the Cleveland Museum of Art, for her help with locating recalcitrant photographic sources.

Finally, this project could not have happened without the enthusiastic support of the art museum's former director Susan M. Taylor. It was her abiding interest in architecture and her commitment to give it visibility in exhibitions that has permitted initiatives such as this. I gratefully acknowledge her encouragement and assistance.

Frank Gehry On Line

An architect's sketch reveals the temperaments
of his or her hand, a lineage of emotion and
gesture into space, for architecture is also a
history of hands. From the piercing certainty
of a Mies line to the lyrical-ethereal pastel
line of Kahn sketches, the lineage of hands
offers a direct linkage to the architect's spirit.

Carlos Jiménez

Of Drawings and Sketches

Architectural drawings are latecomers to history. Until the
Renaissance, most buildings were either conceptualized
with models or built empirically from templates. Moreover,
before paper generally became available in the fifteenth
century, architectural drawings were rare; parchment
was expensive, and it was only during the Renaissance
that drawings began to be collected—first by architects,
and then by connoisseurs.[1] For architects, they were
objects of use value; for the collector, however, they served
as objects of aesthetic appreciation as well as indexes

of symbolic capital. From the nineteenth century on, these
drawings have been collected by institutions such as
museums or government archives, which classify them
and, more recently, exhibit them to the public as works to
be admired in their own right. Today, architectural drawings
have their own institutional clients, which include specialized galleries and art collectors, not to mention that most
ephemeral of modern clients, the auction house.

Gifted architects are not necessarily great draftsmen.
With its phobia of ornament, Modernism has shown a
particularly ambivalent relation to draftsmanship, apprecia-
tive of its qualities but fearful of its excesses. Yet the
early twentieth century produced an extraordinary trove
of great master drawings. In Vienna, the secessionists
close to Otto Wagner cultivated architectural drawing
as an art, and left beautiful, jeweled Klimt-like examples
that even then became collectors' items, aimed un-
abashedly at the market. These were neither preparation
drawings for clients nor loose sketches, but picturesque
perspectives delicately colored in wash or gouache,
with an occasional touch of gold, and clearly meant to
be reproduced in books and magazines. (Adolf Loos's
aversion to drawing may have been in part a reaction
against the graphic glamour dear to his fellow Viennese;

he preferred dealing with models and left no inspired drawings). In Switzerland and France, Le Corbusier produced hundreds of magnificent drawings and polished watercolors in his youth strongly influenced by John Ruskin, as well as pencil drawings in later years. In Germany, the elegance of Mies van der Rohe's reticent sketches and the bravura of Erich Mendelsohn's bold, sweeping lines all left their mark on the profession. In this country, Frank Lloyd Wright's growing fame was greatly aided by his exquisite early drawings (often rendered by the architect Marion Mahony), which were widely published on both sides of the Atlantic Ocean.

The tradition continued in the 1950s and 1960s. Louis Kahn and, above all, Alvar Aalto excelled in this domain, as did still later architects as diverse as Michael Graves, John Hejduk, Léon and Robert Krier, and Aldo Rossi. That so many famous twentieth-century architects distinguished themselves in this field attests to the importance of their training, which was still indebted to the great and much-maligned tradition of the École des Beaux-Arts that enshrined drawing in the famous envois of the Grand Prix. Final renderings, to be judged by the client or competition jury, were so highly prized that architectural draftsmanship became professionalized. Specialists in

drawing—rather than building—architecture appeared, often
attaining great distinction, as the impressive achievements
of Iakov Chernikhov and Hugh Ferriss attest.

Although architectural drawings have been published
since the Renaissance, publications and exhibitions have
different goals and are aimed at different audiences. The
very fact that drawings can be exhibited at all gives them
the imprimatur of artistic value and can influence them
before they are even executed. As John Whiteman points
out, "the rules of drawing and the reception of drawing
may come to determine what is seen and what is drawn."[2]
The drawings of Zaha Hadid were always meant to be
reproduced and displayed. Rendered with exquisite
graphic refinement, they exude a certain theatricality, a
form of address that invites spectatorship. Whether or
not they are shown to the public, their exhibition value
is patent. In our day, most architectural drawings are
generated by computers. Nevertheless, despite the
dwindling number of practitioners, the art of drawing has
survived, especially among those trained before computers
transformed architectural practice.

It was only in the twentieth century that sketches, a more
informal type of drawing, came to be privileged over

more elaborate renderings when modernity conferred
upon them the dubious and elusive notion of authenticity.
Executed freehand and linked indelibly to their makers,
sketches suggest spontaneity and subjectivity, the
immediacy of thought caught on the wing, the wayward
whimsy of the daydream. They thus exceed representation,
and reveal more about their authors than do accom-
plished drawings. Autobiographical traces surface here
and there: the glimmer of half-remembered buildings, of
effects of light and landscape encountered on journeys
past. A form of handwriting, sketches reveal idiosyncratic
ticks and gestures, clues to the architect's personality.
Sometimes close to doodling, they have not severed the
liberating relation to the unconscious.[3]

Finished plans, sections, and elevations, traced on paper
with ruler and compass and pruned of all personal
references, differ significantly from the open-ended
capriciousness of the sketch, still subject to change and
development. Presentation drawings must be self-
explanatory. Armed with all the enhancements of visual
seduction, they are addressed to the client, whether
individual or corporate. They are public rather than
private. So are working drawings, clearly legible road
maps for builders and contractors, who are nowadays

divorced from the architect. Sketches, on the other hand,
depend on an economy of time and, sometimes, money.
Often drawn on odd scraps of paper, sometimes with
several on a single page, they are occasionally left
unfinished. They are impermanent in other ways as well,
quivering uncertainly with irregularities and pentimenti,
shorthand for ideas not yet congealed. They are private
rather than public.[4]

Not all architects appreciate the mercurial unpredictability
of the sketch, the inconclusive work in progress shaped
by doubts and marred by imperfections. A patrician like
Wright disapproved of its impetuous errancy so inimical
to collected thought: "conceive the building in the
imagination, not on paper but in the mind, thoroughly—
before touching paper," he declared archly, every word
cast in stone. "Let it live there—gradually taking more
definite form before committing it to the draughting board.
When the thing lives for you—start to plan it with tools. Not
before. To draw during conception or 'sketch,' as we say,
experimenting with practical adjustments to scale, is well
enough if the concept is clear enough to be firmly held."[5]

Gehry's Sketches

It would be difficult to imagine an architect more different from Wright than Frank Gehry. Wright always focused on the building. Gehry, of a much younger generation, never loses sight of the architect, with all his emotional baggage, his strengths and weaknesses. With Gehry, the distinction between drawings and sketches is tenuous: his most beautiful renderings are unquestionably sketchlike. As sketches have only recently become objects of institutional display, Gehry's sketches, which have been published occasionally but never systematically, have only begun to attract attention in the past decade or so. Small in scale and rarely colored, his hand-drawn études avoid the polish and stylishness that distinguish computer-aided graphics, reveling in their unkempt edges and exuberant free play. But Gehry, too, is subject to the laws of the market, which require art to be exhibited, ultimately affecting its nature: "[M]aybe I'm getting perverse because people have been looking at my drawings, so I haven't been drawing so much. I'm kind of self-conscious about it."[6] There is something enduringly intimate and private about these works even in a museum setting—as if the sketch on display is a confidence revealed.

Years of experience producing presentation drawings for
big architectural firms like Victor Gruen's have left Gehry
with invaluable skills, as well as a strong dislike of the
exacting discipline of traditional draftsmanship: "In the
early days, my drawing techniques were very glib; I spent
time learning renderings and perspectives. I can do those
real well, and I did them as a professional renderer for
people like [John] Portman."[7] At the same time, Gehry's
growing interest in contemporary art led him to question
traditional architectural practice and try his hand at more
intuitive modes of expression. Working with artists opened
his eyes to the power of improvisation, to the poetry of
the unfinished and the elliptical.

After opening his own studio, Gehry weaned himself
from the limitations of standard professional renderings,
and eventually came into his own with an inimitable
style of drawing, a continuous line that roams freely and
playfully with no attempt at objectivity or the faithful
representation of actual buildings. Neither descriptive nor
illustrative, his fluid, footloose sketches depart radically
from accepted custom; one cannot subvert traditional
canons in architecture without undermining conventional
systems of architectural notation. Methods of representation set the parameters for architectural form, and

establish not only what can be said but also *how* it can be said.[8] His new approach virtually suppresses the architectural image in favor of the idea: its aim is not to describe, but to seek and evoke. Whether quick or slow-moving, Gehry's meandering line moves on interminably, like wire in a sculpture by Alexander Calder (fig. 1). In fact, it shares its main characteristics with art. "I've looked at Matisse's drawings and I know the guy doesn't lift his pen off his paper, so maybe I've done that," Gehry acknowledges.[9]

Despite a nod to tradition here and there, all architectural elements are given such an unusual treatment that the viewer cannot identify the familiar elements of wall and roof, door and window. In addition, the architect abstracts a great deal, barely hinting at context and texture. A few vague lines indicate the horizon or the surroundings when they exist at all. It is up to the presentation drawings and final models to give the project a local habitation and a name.

Gehry also departs from established practice in other ways. He has largely abstained from producing the travel sketch—one of the great staples of twentieth-century architects, who replaced historicism's linear

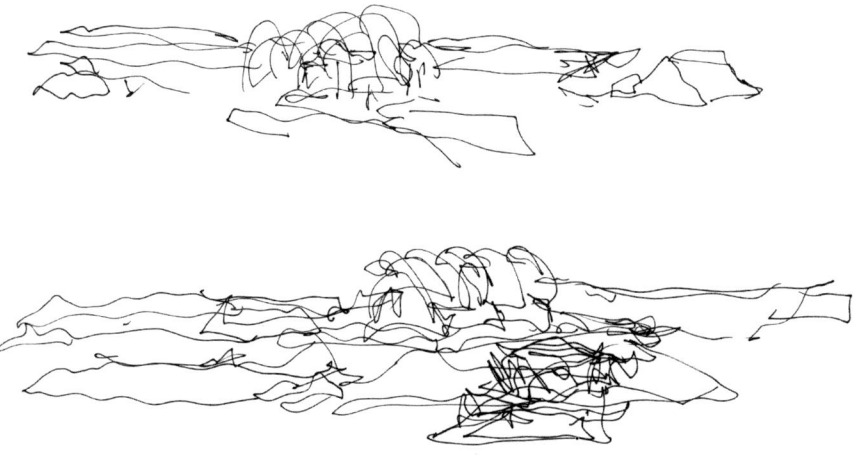

Figure 1. Herman Miller, Inc. Western Regional Manufacturing and Distribution Facility,
Rocklin, California, undated

trajectory through time with a more eclectic and unsystematic trajectory through space. For an architect like Le Corbusier, drawing was an important means of perception, and he built up a personal archive of extraordinary sketches that continuously nourished his designs.[10] Closer to Gehry in time, Aalto and Kahn both left moving records of their voyages in soft pencil and pastel, respectively. Even though Gehry travels a great deal, drawings of buildings seen along the way are rare in his oeuvre and appear only occasionally in his early sketchbooks (fig. 2).[11] On the whole he invokes that other tradition—of contemporary artists who draw from imagination. While Gehry also remembers things he has looked at (how could he not?), his drawings are more inner-directed, less subordinate to buildings actually seen than to other forms of art or visual urban culture.

Drawing is not simply a matter of memory but a medium for thought, a conceptual tool, and Gehry significantly refers to his sketches as a way of "thinking aloud."[12] It is in the act of designing that the architect discovers new possibilities and forecloses others, when the black felt-tip pen, in its interaction with the white sheet of paper, gives shape and form to the thoughts that pressure the hand. Robin Evans, a perceptive authority on

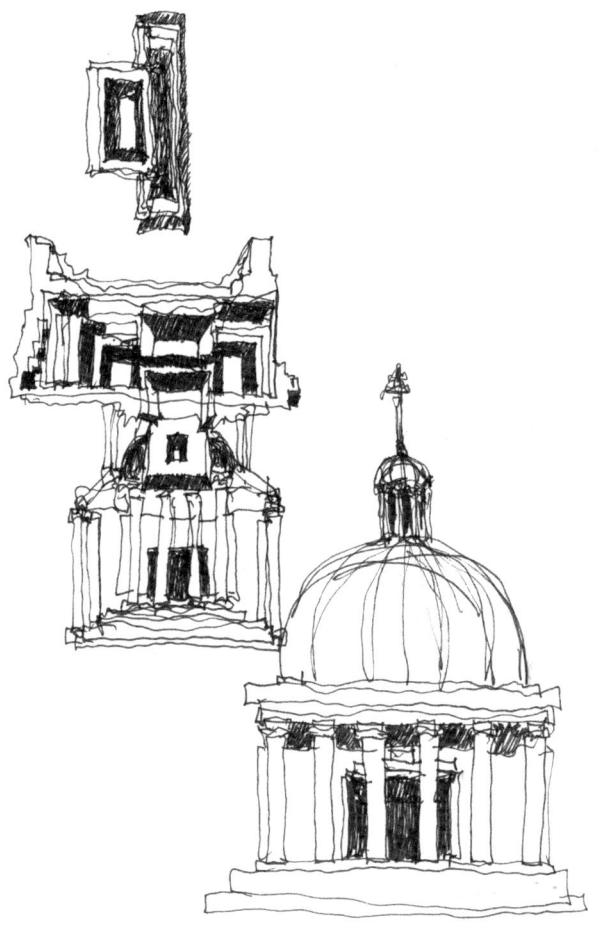

Figure 2. Sketchpad, undated

the subject, argued that architectural drawing "occupies the most uncertain, negotiable position of all, along the main thoroughfare between ideas and things."[13] Unlike finished drawings, sketches are a means for testing intuitions, and are predicated on the primacy of thought over representation. In the indeterminate topology of Gehry's architecture there are no reassuring orthogonals. Euclidean verities can no longer be taken for granted. The same can be said for his sketches, seemingly untouched by exigencies of site and program, or the specificity of materials, their very semiotic instability a sign of freedom (fig. 3). They glory in the urgency of the passing moment, the brief flutter of inspiration. The everyday appears to have no purchase in this realm of fantasy. "Frank says that the only pure image is the sketch, because that comes before anyone else tinkers with it," observed the late film director Sydney Pollack, Gehry's friend of many years.[14] While this is not literally true, the sketch does represent a liberating moment in the search for architectural form before the design has hardened irrevocably into a final option. But it exists in an ambivalent bind, as both the means to an end and an end in itself, as if "the imaginative intelligence of the architect is divided between inventing the drawing and inventing the thing drawn."[15] There are sketches and

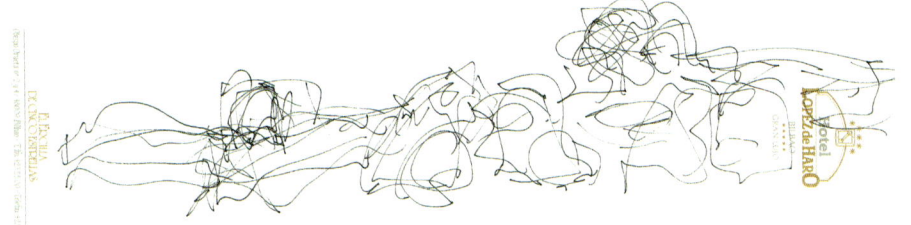

Lewis . F. Gehry

Figure 3. Lewis Residence, Lyndhurst, Ohio, undated

sketches, of course, not all of the same quality. In some, the search for architectural form yields to the aesthetics of drawing itself.

Gehry's peripatetic lines resemble a picaresque odyssey seeking answers across the white expanse of the sheet. As he gropes for the perfect form, trying to anticipate— more or less correctly—the final massing or the final plan, the hesitant empirical nature of the sketch bears witness to an agonizing quest that offers a perch for the viewer's identification. It is just this obstacle course strewn with difficulties, the implacable record of wrong turns and about-turns, that makes the sketch so appealing to modern eyes (figs. 4–5). "I do a different kind of drawing now. They are a searching in the paper," Gehry has observed. "It's almost like I'm grinding into the paper, trying to find the building. . . If you watch me draw—actually draw—you'll see it's a frantic kind of searching. I let that lead, and then make models of the idea scratched out of the paper, and then go back to the drawing, and so on."[16]

The time-bound nature of the sketch offers a sharp contrast to the timeless fixity of the finished building. Sketches are not the result of emotion recollected in tranquility, but the outburst of unruly fantasy, of ideas

tumbling out quicker than the hand can draw. Nothing
should be allowed to arrest the passing train of thought
or cool the burst of entropy. Any hesitation on the part
of the architect destroys the volatility of the idea, the
vision of the inner eye. "'You have to hold the image in
your head while you're doing it," Gehry has remarked,
"and I can't hold the image for longer than 3—I think I
made 3.4 minutes. I clocked it.'"[17] Hence the quicksilver
play of pen on paper, the non sequiturs and dead ends,
the unfinished outlines—a form of shorthand to grasp
thought in motion. Speed is a race against decay,
against the inevitable obsolescence of closure. In its
lack of detailing and small-scale dimensions, the
swiftly drawn sketch permits the architect to keep the
overall image of the project in mind as he subjects
it to constant variations.[18] But speed has another
advantage: it weakens the dependence on the outside
world and keeps the architect tied to the giddy vision
of imagination.[19]

The trace of time recorded in Gehry's mature sketches
also affects the viewers' response to the work as they try
to reconstruct his movements, from the line's inception
on the page to the moment when the pen reluctantly
pulls back from the paper. By leaving behind a "before"

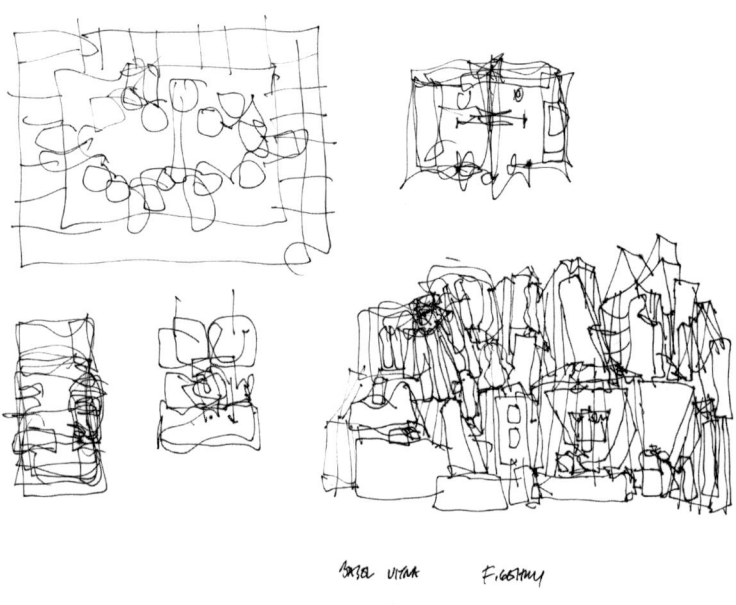

BASEL VITRA   F.GEHRY

Figure 4. Vitra International Headquarters, Birsfelden, Switzerland, undated

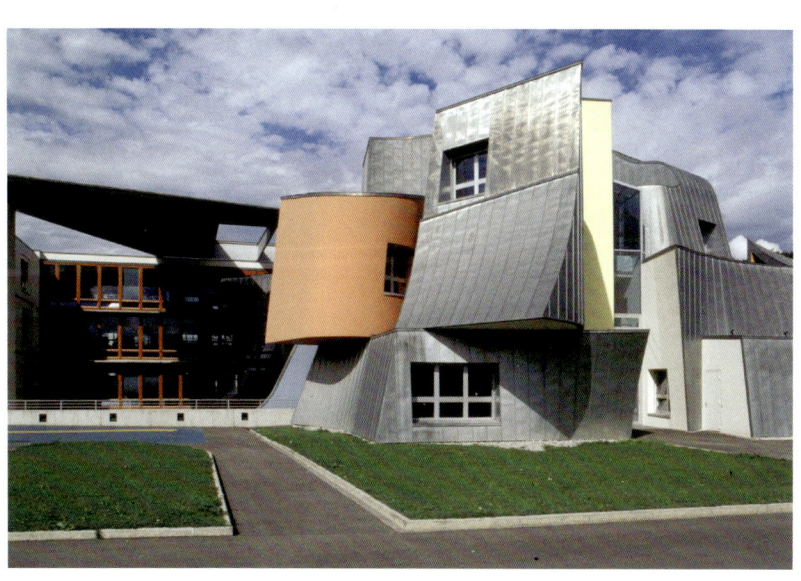

Figure 5. Vitra International Headquarters, Birsfelden, Switzerland, 1994

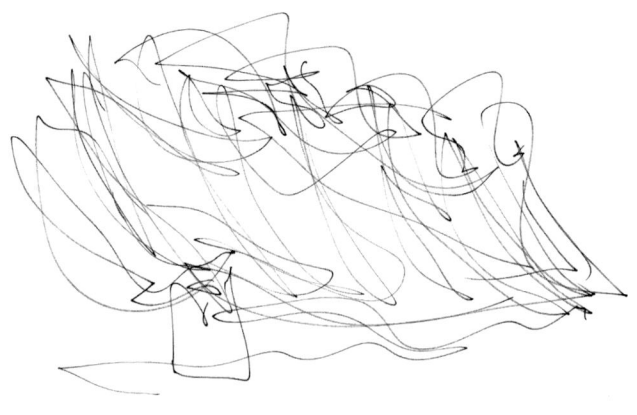

Figure 6. Fondation Louis Vuitton, Paris, France, 2006

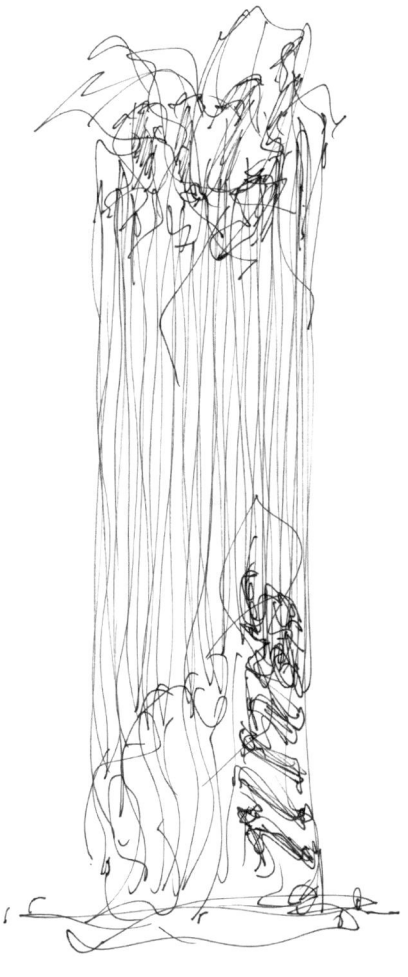

Figure 7. New York Times Headquarters, New York, New York, 2000

and an "after," a trajectory that records the passage of time as well as the articulation of space, Gehry's visual enjambments compel the reader to grasp the image as process (fig. 6). His manner of working differs from the static renderings of most of his peers, in which the drawing exists in a kind of frozen present. The swift meandering line scatters temporal clues in its wake and acquires a gestural, performative aspect, a staccato rhythm that denotes the haste of the hand flying across the paper. As such, a sketch by Gehry constitutes an "ornament of duration," as the poet Paul Valéry once said about dance.[20] Sometimes the pen is allowed to roam unhurriedly, as in the sketches for the *New York Times* headquarters, where the vertical lines must be parallel to each other (fig. 7). By contrast, the elevation for MIT's Ray and Maria Stata Center shows different rhythms, from broad sweeping lines to the pointillism denoting windows (figs. 8–9). Gehry's breathless pace extends beyond the single drawing, since he worked on several commissions at once. Hotel stationary from Bilbao, Spain, for example, reveals that he was engaged with the Lewis Residence (see fig. 3) while at work on the Guggenheim Museum Bilbao. Occasionally, we see different stages of the same project changing before our eyes, like the successive stills of a film (fig. 10).

At the same time, the impulsive, tumultuous act of drawing seems almost like a strategy of deferral, a means for keeping the utilitarian demands of the project at bay and reaching the *parti* too quickly.[21] For Gehry, the liberatory sense of release afforded by the sketch, the impression of seclusion from the pressures of the outside world, is of paramount importance: "You have to find the sculpture in the block of stone. You see it in Michelangelo's Slaves, for example, where he left rough marble untouched. He didn't have a picture to work from, he found the form in the marble. It's the same in my drawings. I have a freedom in my drawings that I love to express in my architecture."[22]

And yet the idea of the autonomous sketch, unfettered by the dross of professional constraints, is misleading. Drawing never emerges out of a tabula rasa, for vision and thought themselves are already stamped by culture and by memory, whether conscious or unconscious. At the back of the architect's mind, program requirements are quietly pressing their case, guiding his hand and prompting his thoughts. Gehry problematizes the relationship between drawing—usually considered a means to an end—and the final architectural product so that one cannot paraphrase his drawings: they are not entirely determined by their referents, as Roland Barthes once said

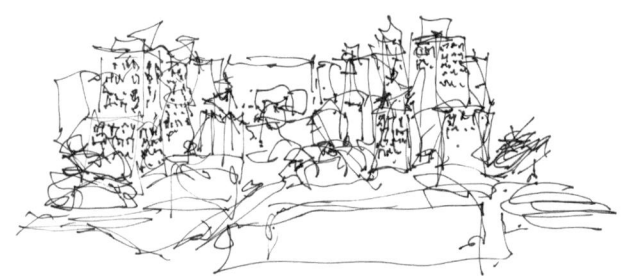

MIT. AUG 99

Figure 8. The Ray and Maria Stata Center for Computer, Information, and Intelligence Sciences, Massachusetts Institute of Technology, Cambridge, Massachusetts, 1999

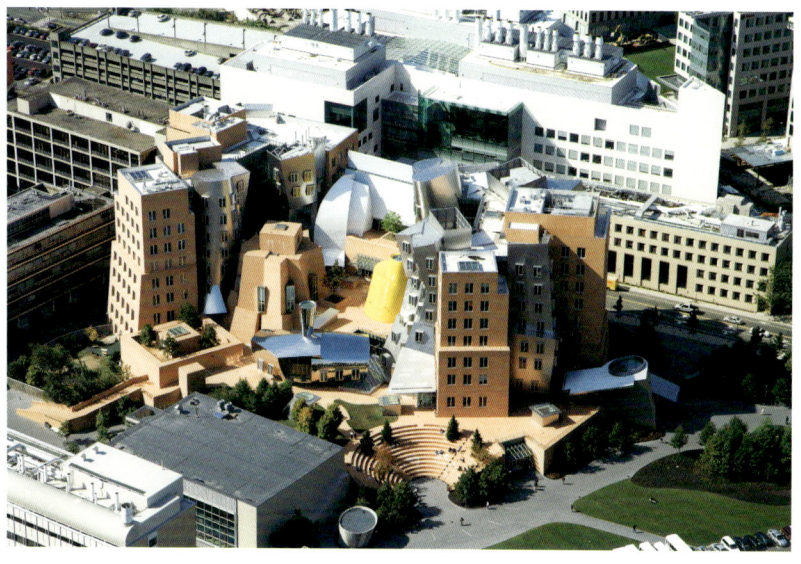

Figure 9. The Ray and Maria Stata Center for Computer, Information, and Intelligence Sciences, Massachusetts Institute of Technology, Cambridge, Massachusetts, 2004

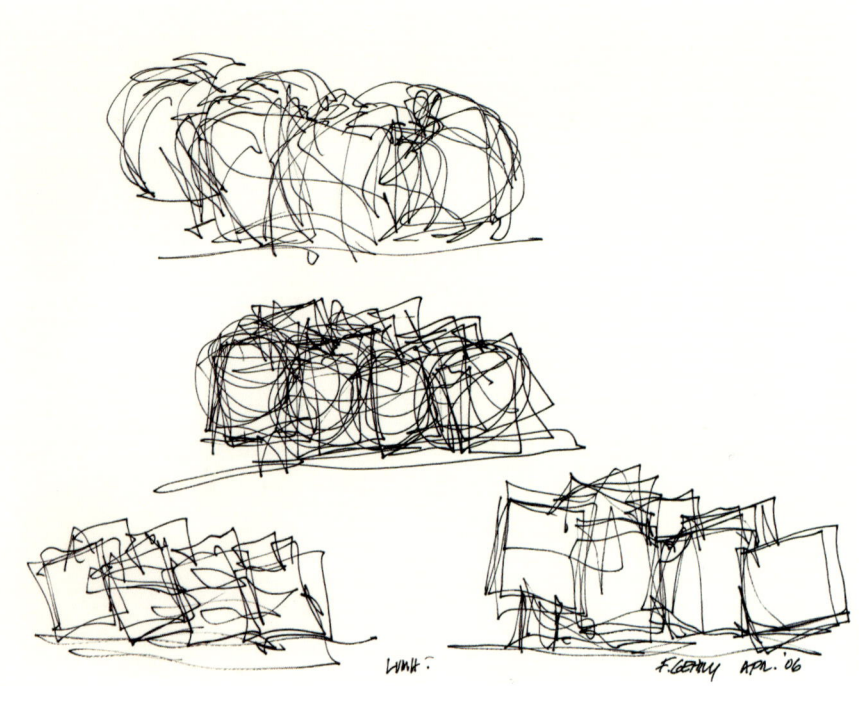

Figure 10. Fondation Louis Vuitton, Paris, France, 2006

of photography.[23] When Gehry begins his sketches, he
does so with the specificity of the program's stipulations
in mind, but in ways that evade the subservience of the
medium to the building. His practice tacitly acknowledges
the ambivalent character of the sketch, the freedom on
which it is predicated, as well as the fact that client, site,
and budget are there from the start, staking their claims.
The architect does not have to resist the image because
it is always informed by programmatic requirements.

In this sense, Gehry's sketches are never simply a record
of automatic writing, as some critics believe.[24] Tradition
itself has not altogether disappeared. Most of Gehry's
sketches are projections—that is, elevations drawn parallel
to the picture plane according to time-honored professional custom. In the past few decades, scholars have
questioned the role of projection and perspective as
vehicles of truth in architecture. Architectural drawings,
including the immaculate renditions handed to the client
at the end of the design process, are not transparent
and value-free. They are representations that come at a
cost, weighed down by a certain amount of ideological
baggage—notably, the pretension to realism, to the way
we see or think we see the world. Although Gehry's
sketches are not guided by the same polemical stance

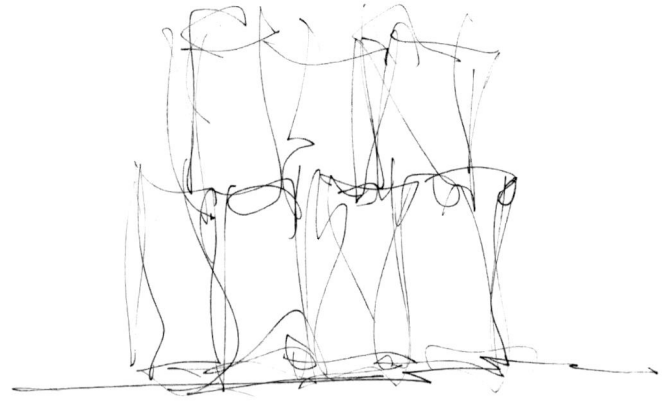

ny. July 05

Figure 11. Interactive Corporation New York Headquarters, New York, New York, 2005

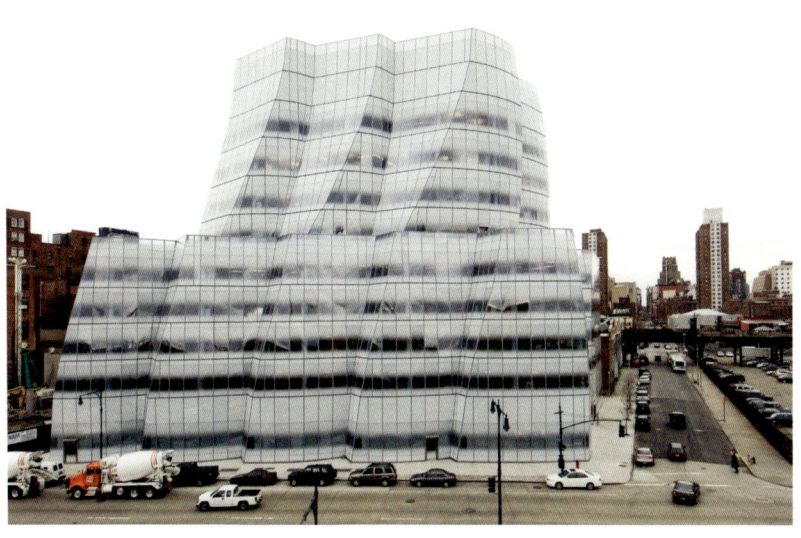

Figure 12. Interactive Corporation New York Headquarters, New York, New York, 2007

that drives his built work, they entail certain epistemo-
logical implications. His whimsical sketches do not try
to pass themselves off as "truth" nor revert to the tricks
of the trade, such as a worm's-eye view that exalts the
building and appears to make it tower over the viewer.
Rejecting mimesis, they assert their otherness in lines
that will rarely be seen in the finished building, even
when it faithfully follows the sketch (figs. 11-12). Like his
architecture, his buoyant, quick-paced sketches express
an eloquent plea for humor and ambiguity (fig. 13). There
seems to be an insouciant ambivalence about Gehry's
sketches that can be read as both two- and three-
dimensional, either as flat lines on a flat sheet of paper
or as lines that cut through a pliant and luminous space.
What he leaves us with are not volumes, but a porous,
permeable extension barely interrupted by the impossibly
thin membranes that attempt to enclose the interiors.
Gaston Bachelard's "poetics of space" acquire a new
dimension in these impalpable buildings glimpsed by
the imagination.

Contours, when they exist, are softened and often
contradicted by the web spun by competing lines, the
skein of black threads that Gehry unravels as he goes
along. The sheet of paper offers no resistance and

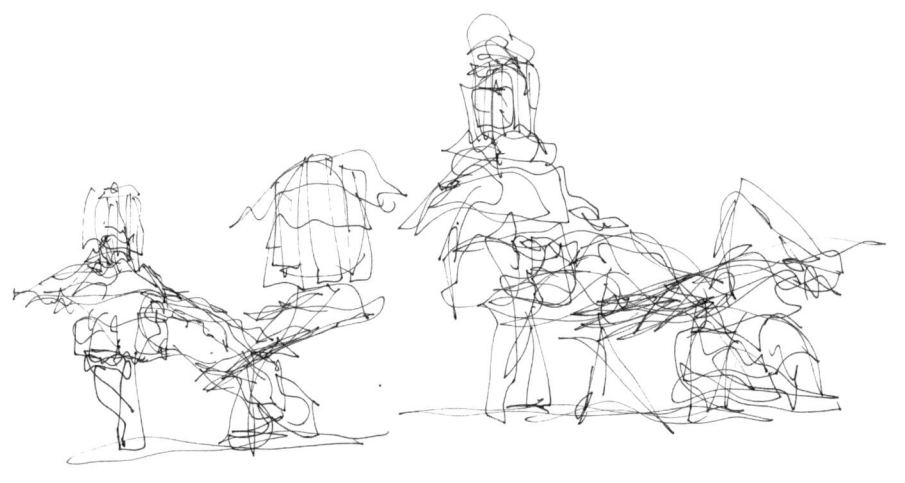

MAGGIES · DUNE '99

Figure 13. Maggie's Centre Dendee, Dundee, Scotland, 1999

dissolves into a transparent medium as the errant line moves across the page, rotates, and circles back, impelled by the flow of ideas. There is something sensuous about the way Gehry goes about his sketches. He clearly relishes the challenge of the slippery surface yielding ground to his interventions: "I love the texture of this paper and I love the fact that you can do this. That I can just go, I never take the pen off. So I would make shapes like this. . . tactile. . ."[25] Sketches empower the sense of touch, as hand and eye constantly relay one another, and the accommodating properties of the haptic temper the cool, detached world of pure visuality. Architect and writer Juhani Pallasmaa elegantly articulates the ways in which the hand confers upon the image something that is more than merely visual. "Even the eye touches," he observes. "Our eyes stroke distant surfaces, contours and edges."[26]

Only rarely do the sketches give us an intimation of Gehry's manner of disarticulating traditional architecture, slicing through the interior and exposing the resultant shards and fractured spaces (fig. 14). Neither the abrupt and deliberate discontinuities between interior and exterior nor the different colors and textures of the building's surfaces (fig. 15) appear in the sketches where

the same atectonic approach prevails throughout, and
the run-on lines lend the work a sense of harmony
that is often disavowed in practice. In a striking bird's-eye
view of Walt Disney Concert Hall, the loose strokes
designate both the new hall and the classical colonnade
of the Dorothy Chandler Pavilion to the right (fig. 16). In
this case, the pen's seamless move from one building to
another exemplifies the architect's intention to knit the
disparate structures of the urban context together by
means of the orientation, size, and disposition of his
masses. When color occasionally makes an appearance, it
does so independently of the building under consideration.
In one of the sketches for the Guggenheim Museum
Bilbao, the red designating the main structure and the blue
for the water are used mainly to clarify the *parti* (fig. 17).
In these drawings Gehry does not attempt to convey the
staggering complexity of his volumetric shells, the
technical joinery required by the architecture; instead,
the drawings appear effortless, fiercely independent, and
refuse to subject themselves entirely to the demands of
a purely architectural nature. It can be said, of course,
that in any project, there is always a wide gap between
the building as it is conceived and as it is built, since
sketch and final building are not commensurate nor share
the same medium. Gehry's sketches, however, push

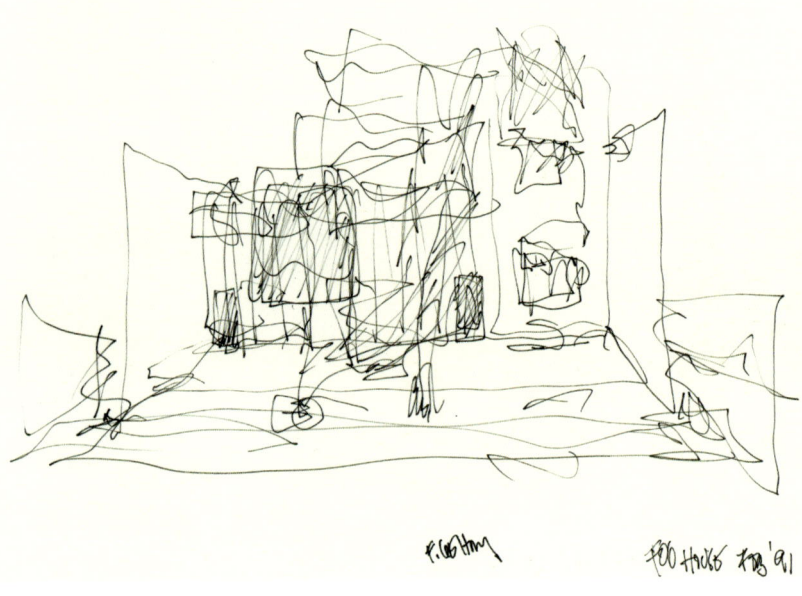

Figure 14. Gehry Residence, Santa Monica, California, 1991

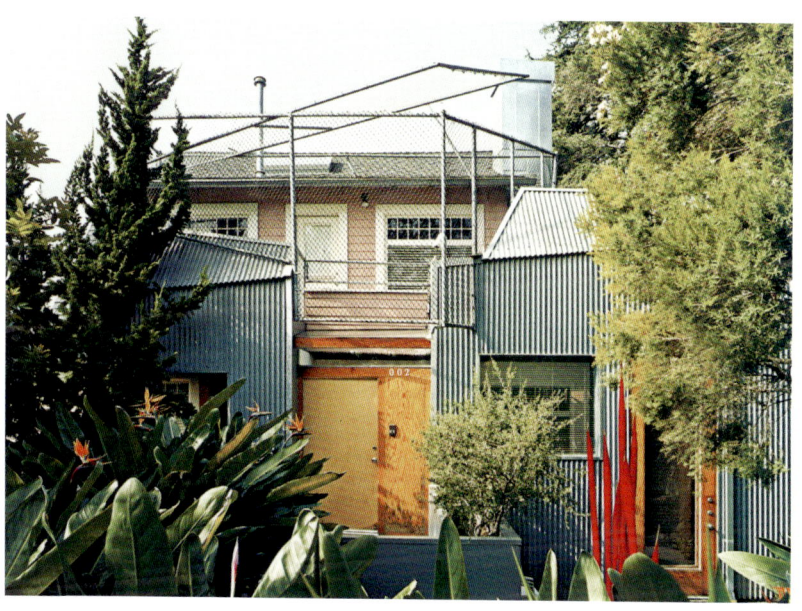

Figure 15. Gehry Residence, Santa Monica, California, 1994

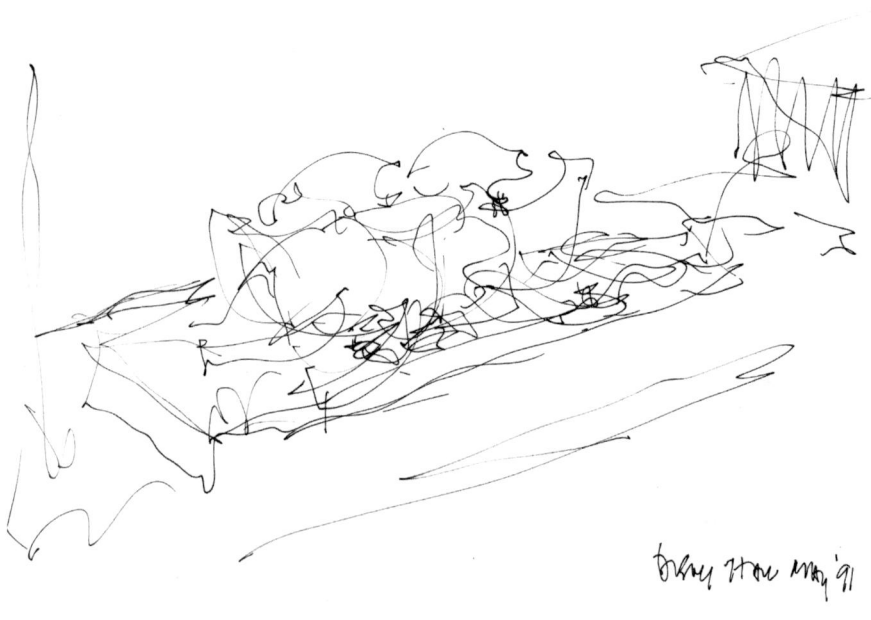

Figure 16. Walt Disney Concert Hall, Los Angeles, California, 1991

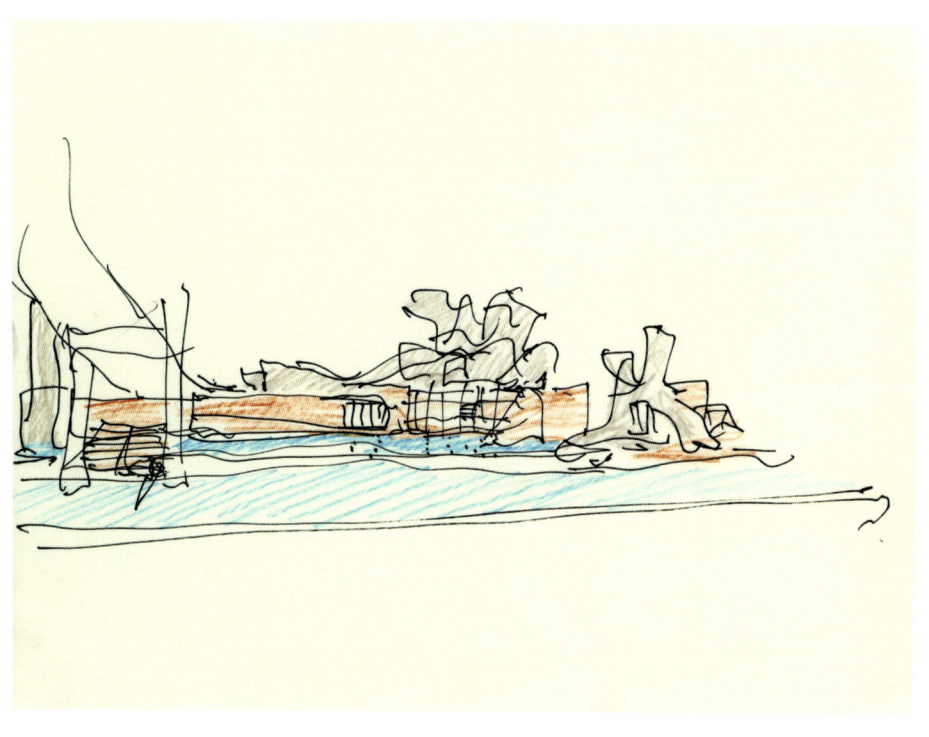

Figure 17. Guggenheim Museum Bilbao, Bilbao, Spain, undated

their independence further still. Despite their refusal to be instrumentalized as mere means, these finely wrought works hover enticingly in the strained and uncertain gap between the ideal world on paper and architecture proper. One cannot divorce the drawings from the architecture any more than one can separate "the dancer from the dance," as William Butler Yeats put it so vividly.[27]

The dialectical relation of the sketch to the final building is something that has always preoccupied Gehry. In his drawings he cultivates the *informe*, loose-jointed look that keeps the work open to evolving possibilities, qualities he likes to impart to his architecture as well (figs. 18–19). "'I am interested in finishing work but I am interested in the work not appearing finished, with every hair in place, every piece of furniture in its spot ready for photographs,'" he has said. "'I prefer the sketch quality, the tentativeness, the messiness if you will, the appearance of in-progress rather than the presumption of total resolution and finality.'"[28] Over the years, however, the cladding on his buildings has changed from a provocative rough finish with common industrial products like exposed wooden studs or the notorious chain-link fence, to the high polish of titanium and brushed steel. More recently, as his drawings have begun to attract attention, Gehry has tried to narrow the breach between the sketch and the building by making architecture submit to the more impromptu side of his practice: "I want everything to look like my drawings," Gehry announced when unveiling the sketches for the Fondation Louis Vuitton, a cultural center to be built in Paris for LVMH Moët Hennessy Louis Vuitton, the purveyor of luxury goods.[29] In this most ethereal of all of his models—construction has not yet begun—the metal skins have been shed in favor of glass; space seems to be synonymous with light (fig. 20). Yet although the model has the ephemeral, diaphanous qualities of a sketch, it does not resemble the architect's drawings for this specific project. Gehry's manner of working does not lend itself to mimesis.

One could say that the new sheathing adopted for high-end clients and institutions no longer leaves room for the serendipity and punning sense of humor of former years, the California beachcomber's aesthetic. A sleek elegance now characterizes all of Gehry's exteriors. In the case of LVMH, the filmy membrane that serves as an exterior no doubt became increasingly refined as the project developed. But one might also argue that as Gehry's architecture has become more genteel his

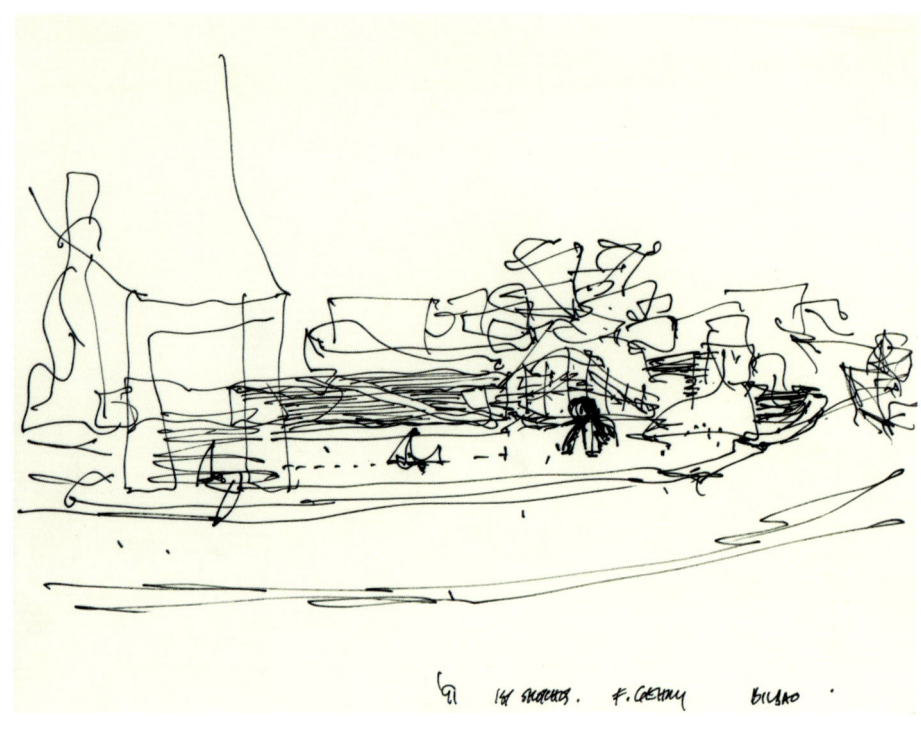

Figure 18. Guggenheim Museum Bilbao, Bilbao, Spain, 1991

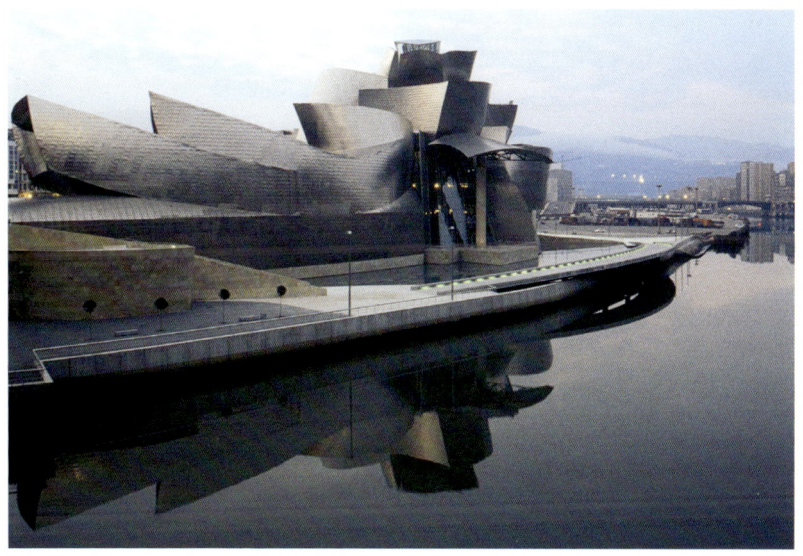

Figure 19. Guggenheim Museum Bilbao, Bilbao, Spain, 1997

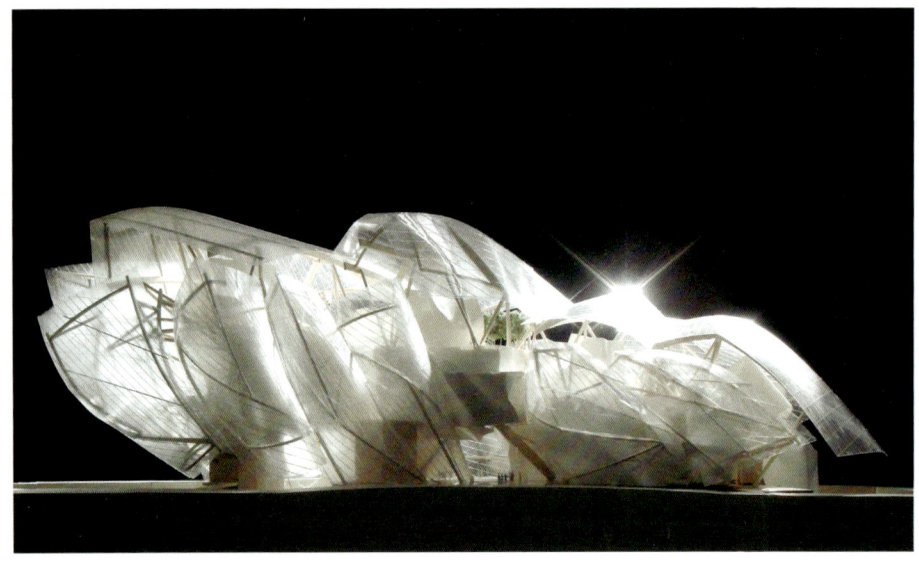

Figure 20. Fondation Louis Vuitton, design process model, 2007

sketches have attained a higher level of sophistication. By ensuring that every form, however complex, can be built to specification, the computer has revolutionized Gehry's architectural practice, and possibly his sketches as well. No longer bound by the need to instruct and inform, his fantasies can soar into the unknown and the unconventional.[30]

Just as the sketch registers the importance of computer technology on one level, so too does it reflect more earth-bound practicalities such as the delicate relation to the client, a notorious source of potential friction. Departing from the norm, Gehry makes use of the client's life and wealth of experiences to prod his own imagination into uncharted territory. This modus operandi gives the architect a broader playing field and helps shape the genesis and development of the drawing: "'So, instead of a house being one thing, it's ten things. It allows the client more involvement, because you can say, "Well, I've got ten images now that are going to compose your house. Those images can relate to all kinds of symbolic things, ideas that you've liked, places you've liked, bits and pieces of your life that you would like to recall." I think in terms of involving the client.'"[31] In his hands, the project, like the sketch, comes close to being a confessional mode, a sort of first-person narration with the architect sometimes speaking for the client as a ventriloquist. The intensity of the interaction does not always work out smoothly, and some collaborations are more rewarding than others. On occasion, Gehry can gleefully act as an agent provocateur, producing drawings and models that are sure to shock the client: "'I'm enough of a voyeur that I like to see how somebody responds to what I do—that is, how they respond to it even if they shriek.'"[32] And clients have been known to shriek.

It is the plan that registers the project's requirements first and foremost. It comes into being early, first sketched out in a very loose way, then slowly taking shape with the help of models. There is a considerable give-and-take between Gehry and his staff, who engage in a dialectical process during which the final design comes into being, by comparing models of different scales with the sketches. While the sketch goes through several different versions that can vary more or less depending on the project at hand, it never actually reaches a finite, finished form as in traditional practice. When the project is complete, Gehry's assistants translate it into computerized form. This manner of working is not too different from the architectural practice of some of the great twentieth-century masters. Aalto, a kindred spirit, also produced exquisite freehand sketches that his chief architect later transformed into plans.[33] Gehry's plans, surprisingly, are given the same exquisite aesthetic treatment reserved for the elevations. They, too, are brought within the pale of art, another instance of the abiding power of the image in Gehry's work and of his iconic bent. Plans are often drawn two or three times so the contours dissolve in a haze of overlapping lines that keep the forms slightly out of focus, slipping from the spectator's grasp. In his wish to avoid massive structures that dwarf their surroundings, the architect often resorts to an archipelago of smaller buildings around an equivocal center that resists stasis. This penchant for centrifugal plans appears in several works, like the Lewis Residence and Princeton University's Science Library (figs. 21–22).

Gehry has developed a kind of architectural notation that allows him to conceptualize the exterior and the interior of his buildings at the same time, as in the sketches for the BioMuseo—Panama: Bridge of Life, Panama City, Panama (fig. 23). Diminutive figures, whose function is to emphasize scale, appear inside and outside the building. Given the complexity of the architectural shell, however, it is extremely difficult to represent Gehry's

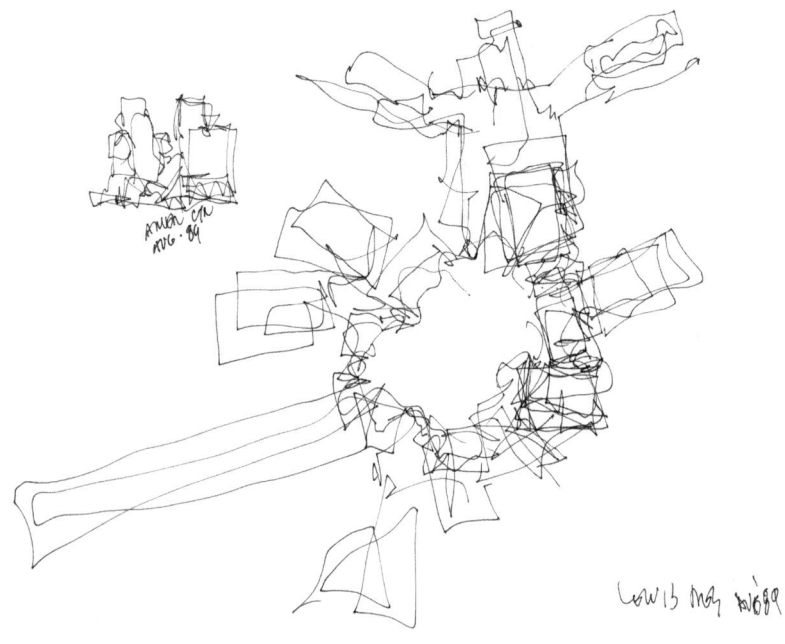

Figure 21. Lewis Residence, Lyndhurst, Ohio, 1989

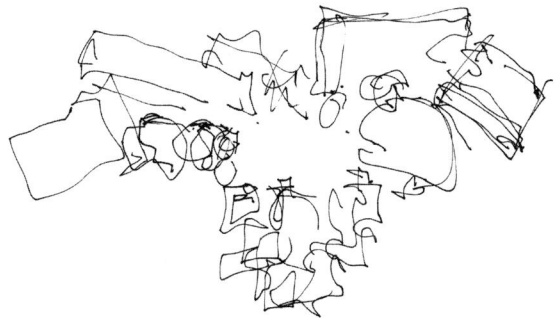

color 200 pm.

Figure 22. The Peter B. Lewis Science Library, Princeton University, Princeton, New Jersey, plan view, 2005

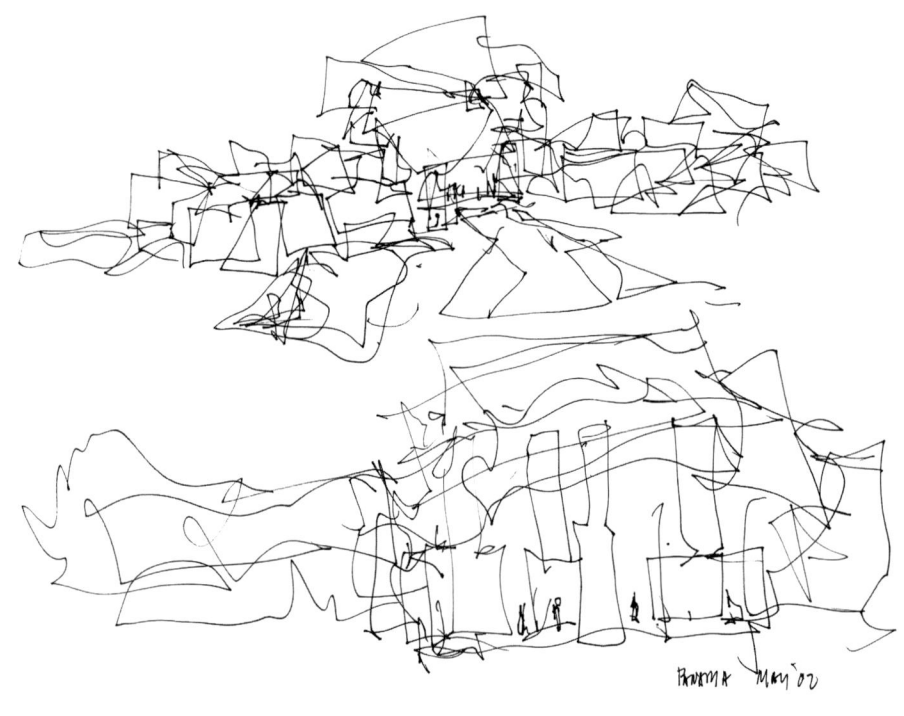

Figure 23. BioMuseo—Panama: Bridge of Life, Panama City, Panama, 2002

interiors with their multiple viewpoints, or even to suggest
the circuitous route of the promenade through the building.
The studio therefore developed a unique way of analyzing
interior space, by moving a tiny camera inside the models
to get a clearer picture that then served as a basis for
further elaboration (fig. 24).[34] There are few sections and
axonometrics among his sketches due to the same diffi-
culty. Only highly specialized, large-scale models and
computer-aided graphics can do justice to the complexity
of Gehry's spaces. This is particularly the case with
projects like MIT's Stata Center or the Panama City
BioMuseo, compressed cities of great intricacy with their
miniature urbanism and interior streets (see figs. 8, 23).

Scale and Model

Another technical aspect addressed by the sketches is
scale. This is all the more important since Gehry eschews
traditional methods of achieving it in his great undulating
masses. Scale is the optimal relation between the parts,
and it situates the human being comfortably within the
architectural shell so that it seems neither too big nor too
small, whatever its size. Everything derives from that initial
ratio between the dimensions of the building and those
of the human figure adopted by the architect, and his
attempt to provide visitors with an empathetic yardstick that

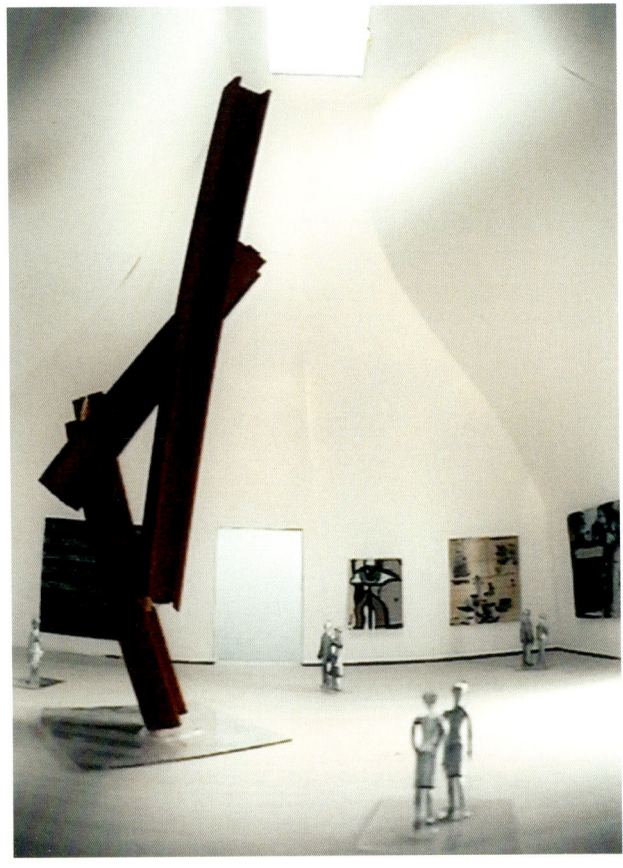

Figure 24. MARTa Herford Museum, Herford, Germany, interior model, 2005

is itself invisible yet patent everywhere. On the exterior, scale has to do with the massing and the openings, with doors and windows and large, glazed surfaces that must not be allowed to dwarf the individual. Inside, whether the room is large or small, some element must be designed to mediate between the dimensions of the building and the size of its tenants. This is particularly important in museums, where huge works of art often share the same space as the spectator (fig. 25). The presence of both plan and elevation on the same sheet (fig. 26) reveals his attempt to do justice to the demands of space without relinquishing a harmonious sense of scale. Gehry has a remarkable grasp on scalar propriety, and several sketches show him honing his design, to ensure a nonthreatening spaciousness (fig. 27). It is here that his biting critique of the corrosive effects of corporate modernism finds its mark, a critique clearly embodied in both his work and his interviews: "I'm a strict modernist in the sense of believing in purity, that you shouldn't decorate. And yet buildings need decoration, because they need scaling elements. They need to be human scale, in my opinion. They can't just be faceless things. That's how some modernism failed. When it started getting used by the developers, it became faceless. It became a language that self-destructed. What was missing was human scale."[35]

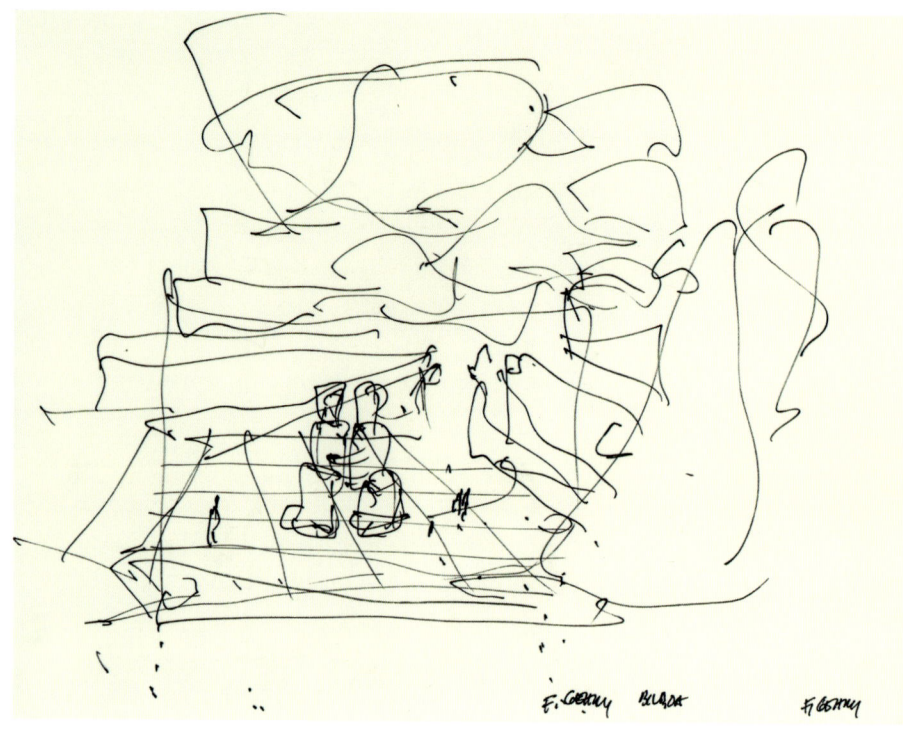

Figure 25. Guggenheim Museum Bilbao, Bilbao, Spain, undated

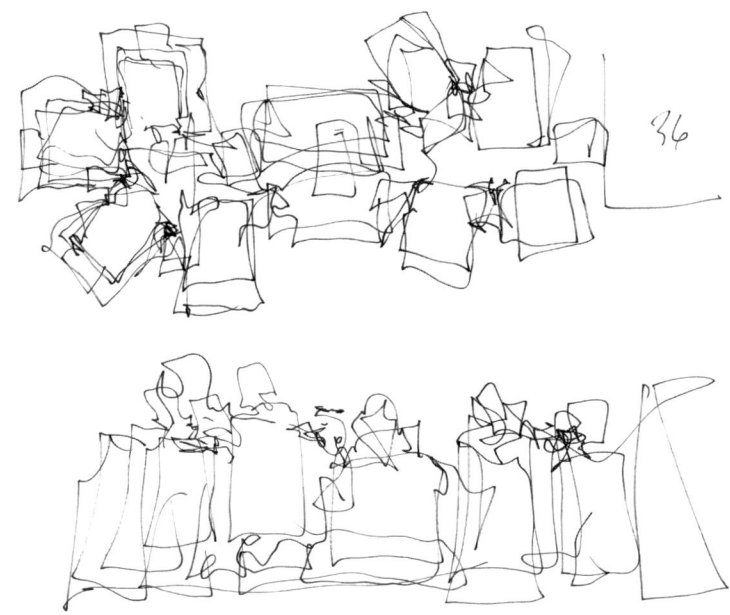

36

MIT. Gehry '98

Figure 26. The Ray and Maria Stata Center for Computer, Information, and Intelligence Sciences, Massachusetts Institute of Technology, Cambridge, Massachusetts, plan and elevation views, 1998

After studying the actual site and the site model, and lengthy discussions with the clients, Gehry sketches the embryo of what in the course of a long and arduous process eventually becomes the final project. Based on these first drafts his staff prepares a certain number of models, as unorthodox as the sketches, and at different scales. Gehry proceeds dialectically from sketch to model and back again as often as needed, and in collaboration with the members of the project team. This manner of working calls for sharp analytical skills, and the ability to shuttle between two- and three-dimensional constructs designed to varying scales, using one medium to goad the other into shape. Models allow him to keep the program, the scale, and the connection to the site in sharp focus as he seeks the final form. "'I always build two models,'" he comments; "'one big, one small, which show a project's program in relation to its city, because if you only work with one scale you become fascinated with the forms for their own sake. You have to force yourself to change scale and go back and forth. It keeps you honest.'"[36] Complex projects, however, require far more models— between thirty or forty in some cases—before the final version is reached.

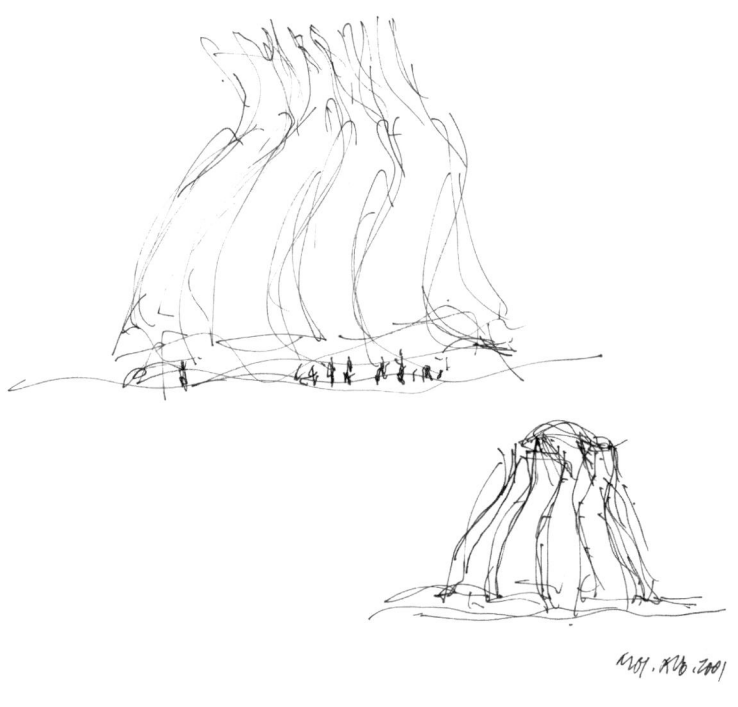

Figure 27. Jerusalem Museum of Tolerance — Center for Human Dignity, a Project of the
Simon Wiesenthal Center, Jerusalem, Israel, Grand Hall, 2001

Initially, models are no more than tentative constructions in various materials—foamcore, wood, paper—that respond to a specific commission and its immediate environment, the urban or natural site on which it is to rise. In the course of the design process they evolve steadily until they finally culminate in the detailed presentation models shown to the client (fig. 28). The exact relation between sketches and models varies depending on the building under consideration. "'How do I use the drawings?'" asks Craig Webb, the project designer for Princeton University's Science Library. "'I'll get a copy and put it on the table. Frank describes what it is. So it's both verbal description and the drawing of a gesture. And then I try to get the energy of the gesture in the drawing. It's tricky because some-times the drawing has a lot more movement than Frank actually wants, and sometimes less. [. . .] We usually work in a sequence: first the drawings, then a model, then Frank looks at the model, evaluates it, and then makes more drawings. Then we make more models. And so on.'"[37]

Process

Since Gehry works with unprecedented shapes and materials, pushing the technological envelope in all

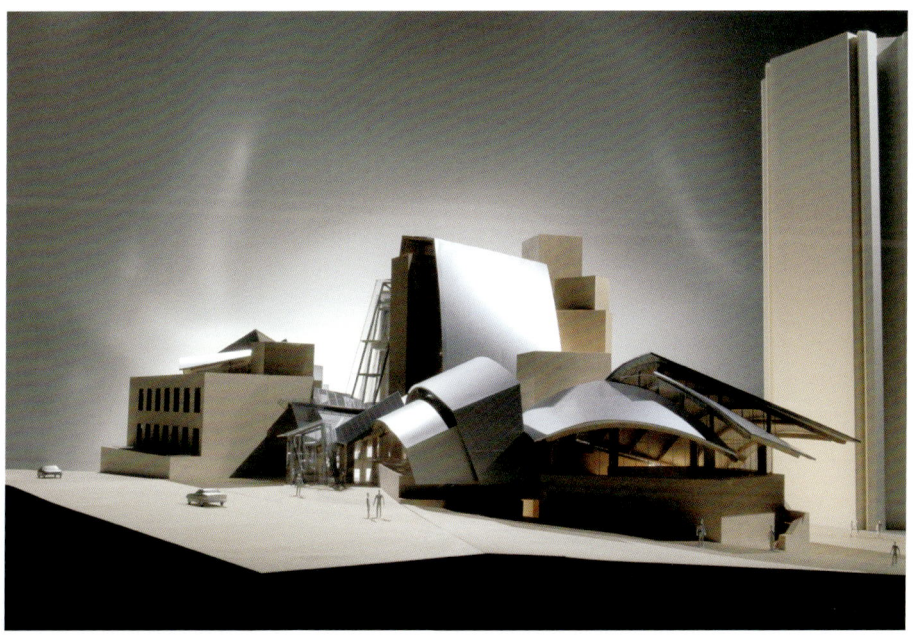

Figure 28. The Peter B. Lewis Science Library, Princeton University, Princeton, New Jersey, final design model, 2003

directions, sketches and models depend on computer-
generated renderings to be translated into viable forms.
Jim Glymph, a former partner in the firm and an expert in
this field, found what was needed in a program produced
for the French aerospace industry by Dassault Systèmes:
CATIA, or Computer-Aided Three-Dimensional Interactive
Application. The images produced by CATIA are themselves striking (figs. 29-30). This software permits the
complex curves of Gehry's models to be digitized, giving
contractors a more accurate sense of feasibility and costs,
and releasing the architect from the need to impart more
detailed information with his drawings. Like other contemporary architectural studios, Gehry Partners depends on a
close collaboration between members of the design team,
who produce sketches, models, presentation drawings,
and digital models. In the domain of architectural representation, Gehry thus occupies the two ends of the
spectrum: if his sketches so often resemble works of art it
is not out of nostalgia for the past, since his office has also
pioneered the most advanced software in the business.
The two are causally linked. He himself never uses the
computer because, as he put it, it "'dries out the ideas, it
takes all the juice out. The computer graphics is [sic]
really an impediment to me. And the reason it's painful is
you look at the computer screen, you see that image

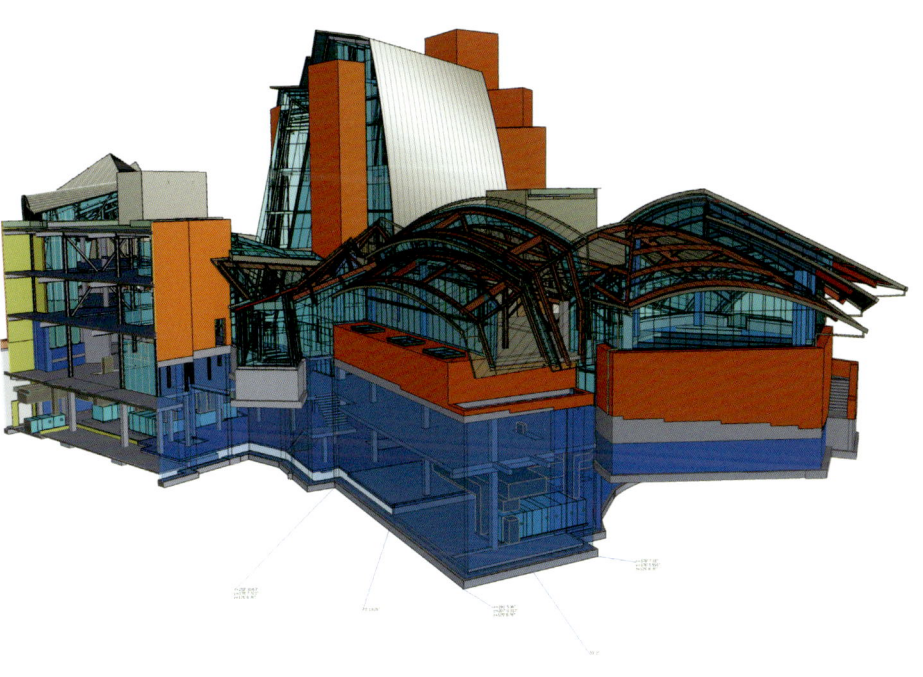

Figure 29. The Peter B. Lewis Science Library, Princeton University, Princeton, New Jersey, digital project master model, 2004

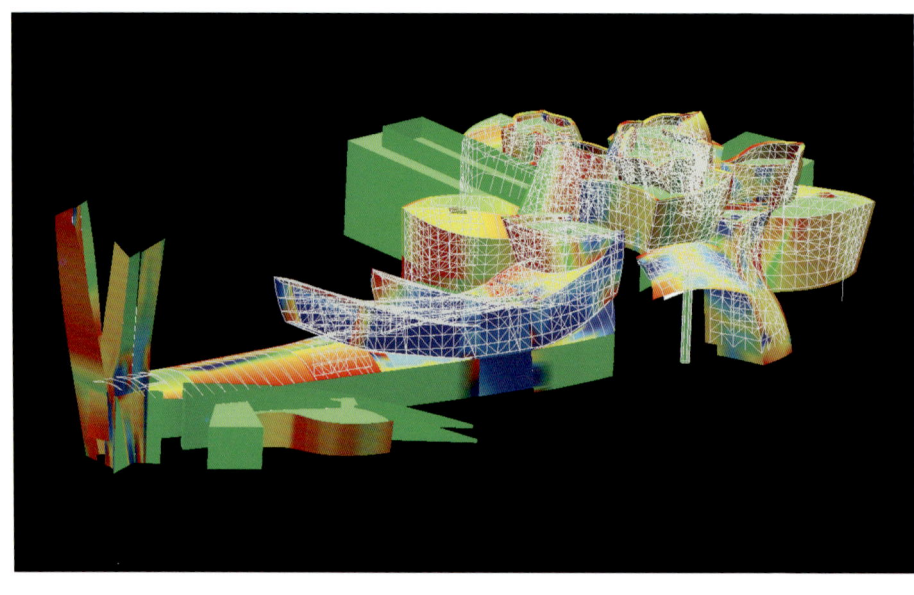

Figure 30. Guggenheim Museum Bilbao, Bilbao, Spain, digital project master model

which is like a dried out version of what you're thinking, you have to hold the dream image in your mind while you're manipulating the thing on the screen which is horrible, and it's very hard, it's excruciatingly painful to carry this image while you're looking at a bad image.'"[38]

Art

Perhaps more than any other architect of our time, Gehry has actively engaged with the art world, constantly collaborating with artists and museums, and deliberately overstepping professional boundaries: "'My approach to architecture is different," he confesses. "'I search out the work of artists, and use art as a means of inspiration. I try to rid myself, and the other members of the firm, of the burden of culture and look for new ways to approach the work. I want to be open-ended. There are no rules, no right or wrong. I'm confused as to what's ugly and what's pretty.'"[39] In the early years in Los Angeles, his greatest support came from local artists and sculptors, and in time he became acquainted with virtually every major figure in the art scene of the 1960s and 1970s, like Chuck Arnoldi, Larry Bell, Billy Al Bengston, Ron Davis, Robert Irwin, Ed Moses, Kenneth Price, and Edward Ruscha. On the East Coast his large circle of friends included Jasper Johns, Robert Rauschenberg, Andy Warhol, and—most notably—Minimalist sculptors like Carl Andre and Donald Judd whose lapidary, three-dimensional oeuvre challenged Gehry's own work on many fronts. Another sculptor of great importance to Gehry's work is Richard Serra, with whom he has collaborated on several projects.[40] For the Guggenhiem Museum Bilbao, Gehry designed a special hall to house works by Serra, and in the Science Library at Princeton University he took into account the orientation of Serra's large steel sculpture *The Hedgehog and the Fox* that adjoins it. Serra's huge pieces have something in common with architecture, while Gehry's buildings have a sculptural dimension.[41] Gehry has also cooperated with Claes Oldenburg and his wife Coosje van Bruggen on built and unbuilt commissions, and more recently with the artist Sophie Calle, another old friend. Inevitably, the architect has drawn different and even conflicting lessons from artists of such diverse tendencies. If Johns and Rauschenberg, for example, taught him to use or expose commonplace materials shunned by the architectural profession, and Pop art to explore the raunchy commercial vernaculars of urban culture (see figs. 14–15), Minimalism encouraged a new sobriety, a concern for crisp, sharp-edged prisms that one sees, for example, in Gehry's long horizontal facade of Team Disneyland's Administration Building in Anaheim,

California (figs. 31–32). Gehry's works, sketches included,
fall between these two extremes of all-inclusive extro-
version and laconic restraint.

When asked which painters influenced him the most,
the architect first mentions Mark Rothko and Jasper
Johns, but then adds, "'Of the Modern, I mean I look at
everybody. Matisse. Picasso. Everybody. I have always
loved stuff that I find in museums, and I would get
excited.'"[42] In his first studio in Santa Monica, California,
itself an unusual museum of sorts, Gehry worked
surrounded by art. Large canvases by Ron Davis and
Ed Moses hung on the walls, as well as lithographs
by Frank Stella; a three-dimensional piece by Larry Bell
shared the floor space with a huge stake painted by
Chuck Arnoldi.[43] Since the 1960s, Gehry has designed
several ingenious art installations for the Los Angeles
County Museum of Art (LACMA), the Museum of
Contemporary Art in Los Angeles, the Guggenheim in
New York, and the Museum of Decorative Arts in
Montreal, among others. He has become a master at
situating art in space, an experience that has served
him well as a designer of numerous museums and, at
least once, as curator. When Gehry's new Weisman
Art Museum in Minnesota opened to the public in 1993,

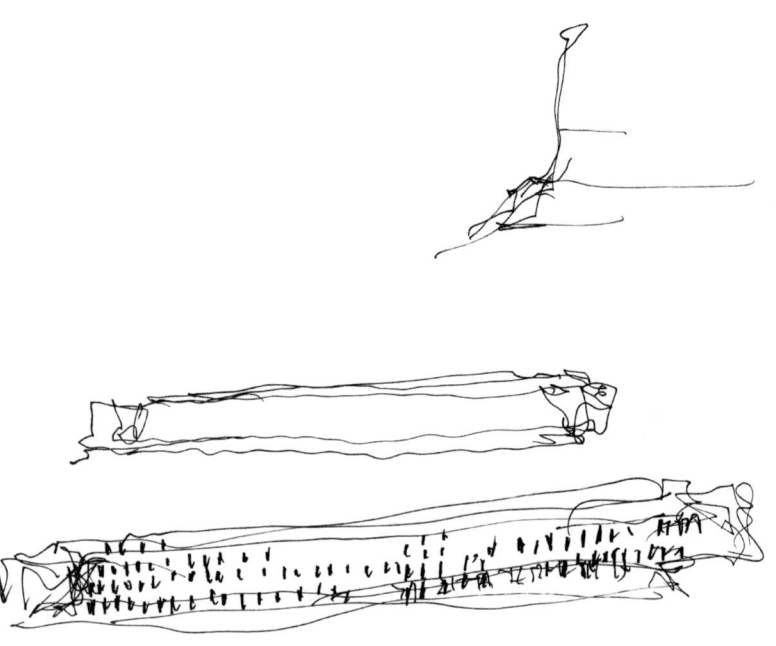

Figure 31. Team Disneyland Administration Building, Anaheim, California, 1992

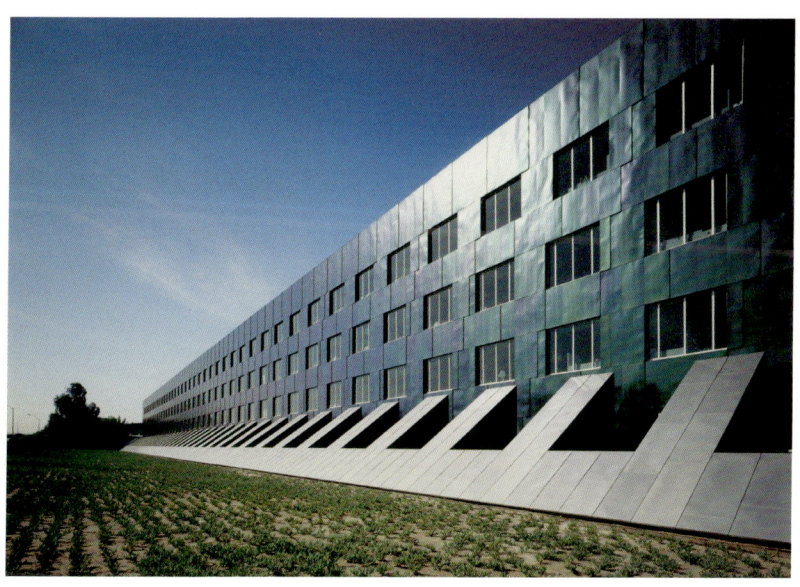

Figure 32. Team Disneyland Administration Building, Anaheim, California, 1995

he was asked to curate its inaugural exhibition and chose, significantly, to display artists whose work resonated most strongly in his own architecture, including Bengston, Davis, Judd, Moses, Oldenburg, and Stella.[44] He has also been on the other side of the divide, as the subject of retrospectives in major institutions like the Weisman or the Guggenheim.

Gehry's connection to art history is more complicated than his relation to contemporary artists. Like the museum, it, too, has served as a catalyst for Gehry's architectural sketches and buildings. At the University of Southern California, where he began as an art major, Gehry followed art history classes with enthusiasm.[45] When he switched to architecture, however, he found that history was anathema to the more dogmatic strains of Modernism. In a way, for the rest of his life he tried to compensate for this lacuna in his education. In 1961 he spent a year in Paris working for the architect André Remondet, and visited some of Europe's great museums and architectural landmarks. Bavarian Baroque, Gothic, Modern, and— above all—Romanesque architecture aroused awe and a certain amount of anger: "I went to Europe, was shocked to find the great architectural history that was [. . .] denied us in school."[46] Gehry's travels and education gave him a literacy in the history of art that gradually found its way into his projects, which always opposed the kind of recessive architecture that can be ignored as background or white noise. Good buildings should make it impossible for the spectator to take them in distractedly, which is the fate of most architecture, according to Walter Benjamin.[47] In order to give back to architecture a strong urban presence Gehry sought inspiration in art: "The *Charioteer of Delphi* [. . .] evokes feelings even though he stood there. It made me cry. There is something poignant that cuts through the bullshit. If those artists can do that in their material then architecture made of material can also [. . .]evoke feelings. Is there a way to use, to evoke feelings within the constraints of budgets and program?" he asks; "can you evoke feelings like the *Charioteer of Delphi*?"[48] Gehry's sketches and buildings attempt to answer the question with their powerful, agonistic forms aimed at imparting affect to architecture (figs. 33–34).

Obviously, figurative painting and sculpture by old masters or contemporary artists do not translate easily and unproblematically into architecture or architectural drawings.[49] Sometimes it is the space between the figures in a canvas that attracts Gehry's attention and leads him to

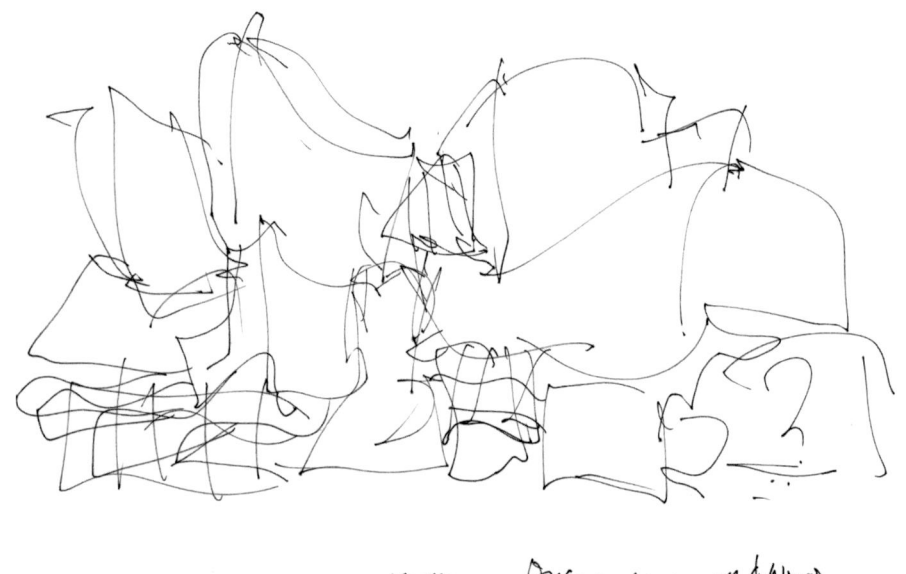

Figure 33. Walt Disney Concert Hall, Los Angeles, California, undated

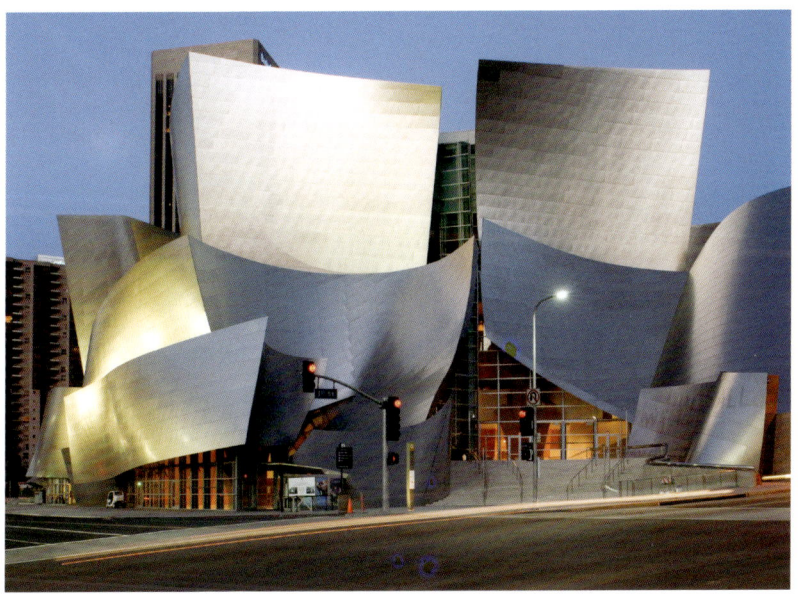

Figure 34. Walt Disney Concert Hall, Los Angeles, California, 2003

mull over analogous solutions in his field. At times, an
unusual form suggests a strategy that can be used, with
the requisite changes in scale and material, in a different
medium: the source for the great cowl-shaped pavilion
of the Lewis Residence (fig. 35) can be found in one of
the mourners of Claus Sluter's *Tomb of Philip the Bold* in
Dijon (fig. 36).[50] Modern art has also sustained Gehry's
relentless questioning of architectural form. In 1980 his
installation of the exhibition of Russian Constructivist art
for LACMA reinforced his interest in the Soviet avant-
garde, patent in earlier works like the Spiller Residence
in Venice, California, or the project for the Familian
Residence. In *Der Neue Zollhof* (The New Customs
Complex), Gehry's housing project for Düsseldorf,
Germany, mass is broken down into smaller units so that
the resulting group of buildings resembles small Tuscan
towns such as San Gimigniano, with their cluster of
baronial towers (figs. 37–38). Yet the same project also
has a more modern source in the art of Italian painter
Giorgio Morandi. "'Düsseldorf is a 'Morandi' project,'"
notes Craig Webb; "'it's a still life, stacked bottles. The
shapes are trying to be sculptural, like bottles in a
Morandi painting.'"[51] Gehry's interest in Morandi has a
wonderful symmetry to it inasmuch as the Bolognese
painter's tightly knit compositions with jars and bottles

were first drawn in plan, and have been compared to miniature architecture (fig. 39).[52]

In each of these projects the original impetus came from several directions at once. Art helped Gehry resolve one aspect of the building, usually having to do with the massing or the general conception of the work. In the case of the Fondation Louis Vuitton in Paris (see figs. 6 and 20), Gehry pursued a preoccupation that had absorbed him for years: how to convey change and movement in a structure that is after all static. He drew inspiration from the scudding clouds of John Constable: billowing, evanescent shapes that refused to coalesce into fixed or final form, and bore the notation of the exact time in which they were executed, the orientation of the wind, and the effects of sunlight. "The idea is of a cloud made of glass," Gehry explains in reference to this project. "The French are famous for their work in glass, so that's exciting. It's difficult to achieve in architecture, but we're getting there."[53]

If Gehry's architecture is often nourished by art that ranges over several centuries, the sketches themselves are closer to modern and contemporary art. The masterful drawings for the headquarters of Vitra International

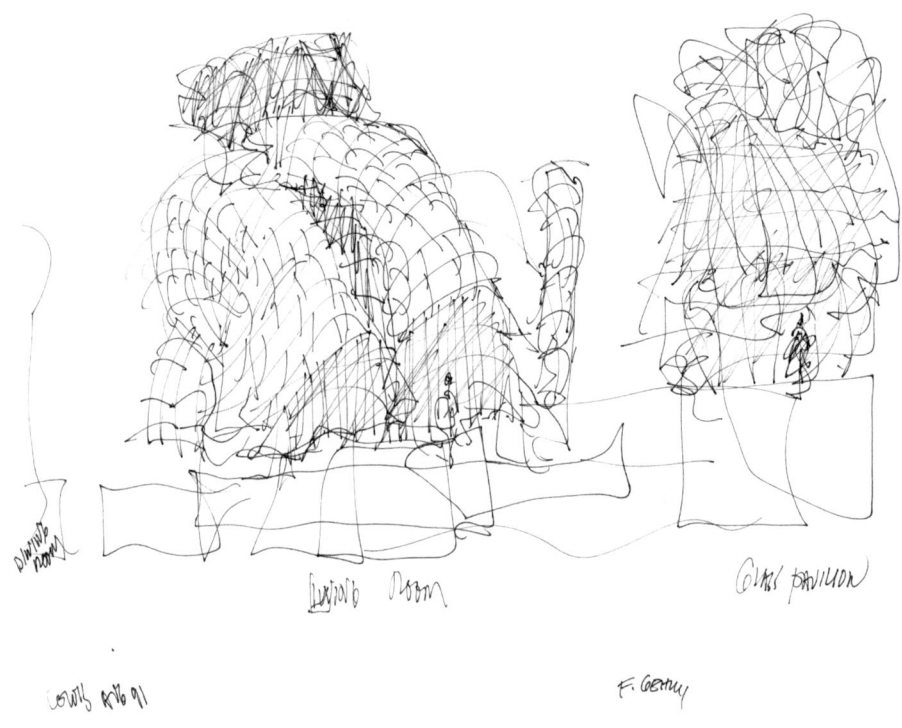

DINING ROOM

LIVING ROOM   GLASS PAVILION

GEHRY APR 6 91   F. GEHRY

Figure 35. Lewis Residence, Lyndhurst, Ohio, 1991

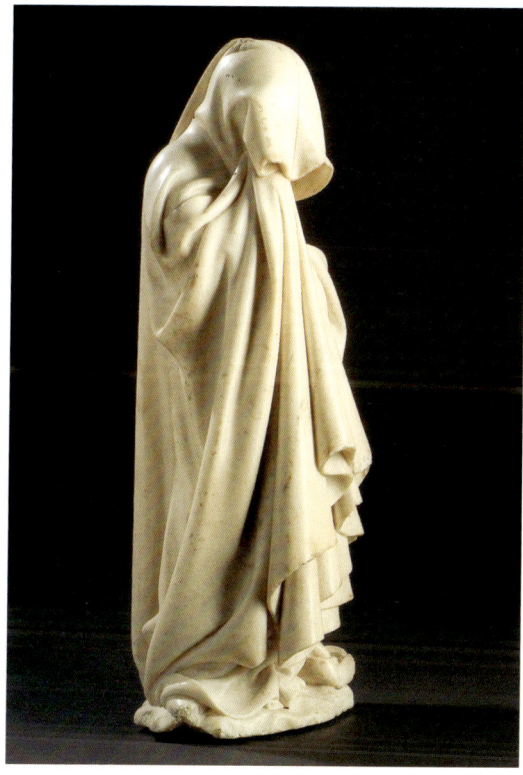

Figure 36. Claus Sluter, Netherlandish, active in Burgundy, ca. 1360–before 1406, and Claus de Werve, Netherlandish, active in France, died 1439. *Mourner No. 21 from the Tomb of Philip the Bold*, 1404–10. Marble; h. 41.0 cm. Musée des Beaux-Arts de Dijon (CA 1416 n° 21)

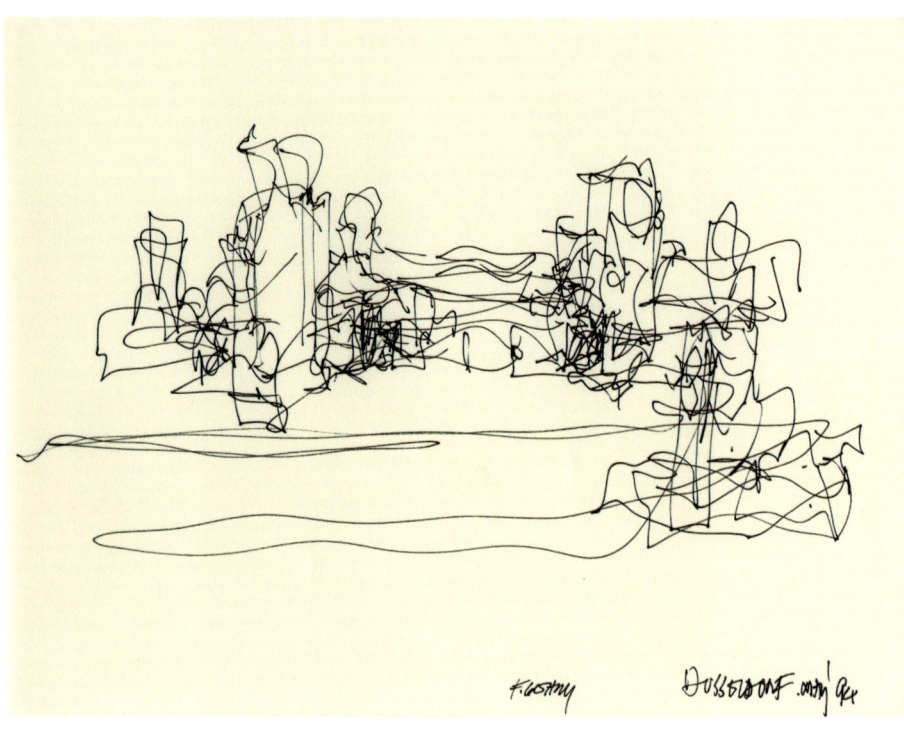

Figure 37. Der Neue Zollhof, Düsseldorf, Germany, 1994

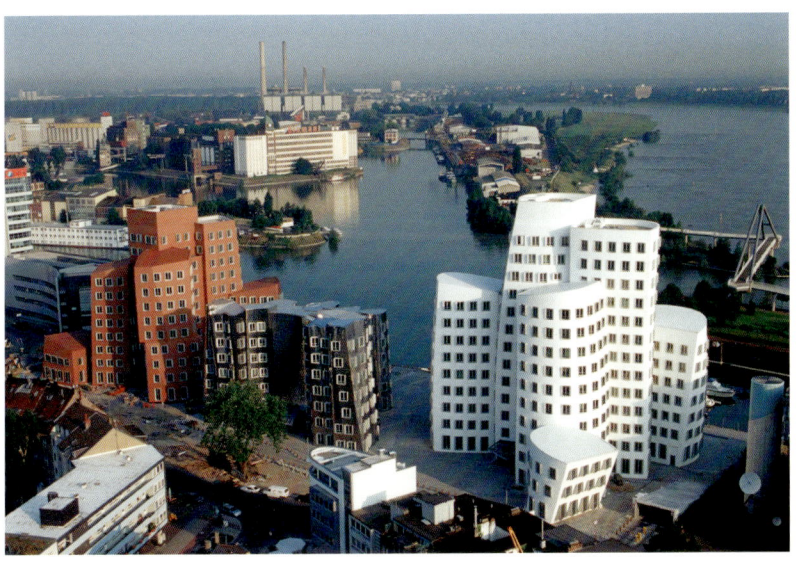

Figure 38. Der Neue Zollhof, Düsseldorf, Germany, 1999

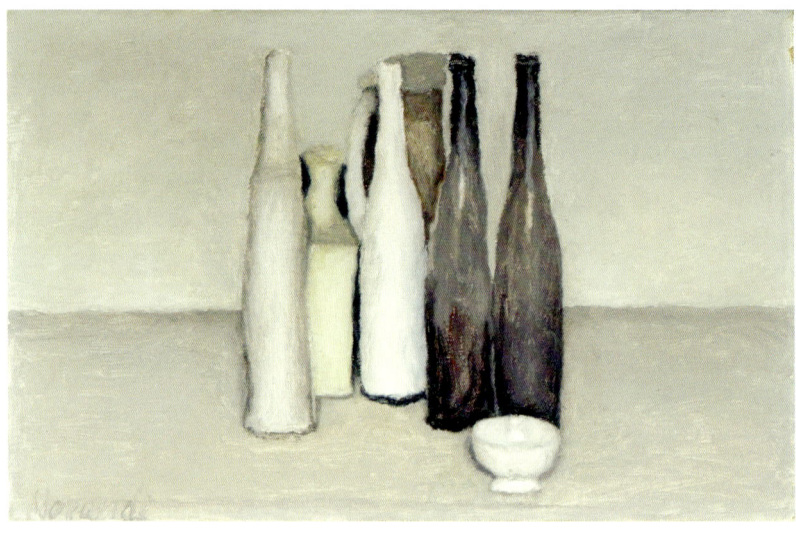

Figure 39. Giorgio Morandi, Italian, 1890–1964. *Still Life*, 1957. Oil on canvas; 25.5 x 40.0 cm. Princeton University Art Museum, bequest of Clinton Wilder, Class of 1943 (y1986-74)

at Birsfelden, Switzerland (see fig. 4), show Gehry's interest in the ludic and seemingly untutored forms of draftsmanship that one finds, for example, in the work of Paul Klee. It is again modern art that informs the elevation for the unbuilt Museum of Tolerance in Jerusalem with its airy, gossamer threads, the tumult of arpeggios on the left contrasting with a more tranquil movement on the right (fig. 40). The twists and turns of the pen show that Gehry is, after all, a contemporary of Cy Twombly, reveling in the virtuosity of alliterating lines and the sheer pleasure of drawing. Similar fugue-like arabesques inform the other sketches of the same project, which bears a certain resemblance to the Princeton University Science Library that followed it closely in time (figs. 41–42). Sketches like these have dual citizenship in the realms of both art and architecture.

Modernity also permeates the elegant sketches for the University of Toledo Center for the Visual Arts, a sustained exercise in abstraction unprecedented in Gehry's work (fig. 43). His ability to lay bare the connection to the site and capture the essential characteristics of the massing with a few terse strokes of the pen, sketched with unfaltering assurance, is a tour de force. Drawing, as they say, is what you leave out. The studied reticence of the design,

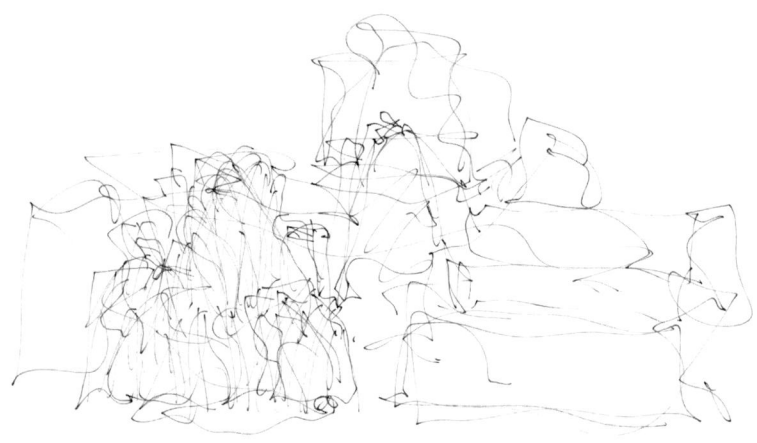

Figure 40. Jerusalem Museum of Tolerance—Center for Human Dignity, a Project of the Simon Wiesenthal Center, Jerusalem, Israel, 2001

and the way it espouses the blank space of the paper to achieve its effect, has the taut refinement of a haiku. Aalto's beautiful and barely figurative sketches come to mind, hovering just this side of abstraction. Very different in style and feeling are the drawings for the Experience Music Project in Seattle (fig. 44), with their numerous pentimenti and tangled webs of sinuous lines. In these Gehry lets out slack like a good fisherman. The contrast between the astringent sketches for the University of Toledo and these spirited lines luxuriating in excess and redundancy show the architect's stylistic range. Each project has a different function that not only determines the building's overall conception but is reflected in the very style of the preparatory drawings.

Gehry's artistic genealogy is complex. What affects his buildings does not necessarily speak to his sketches, which are often beholden to other tutelary gods. On the whole his drawings are far more responsive to art than to the architectural history that sometimes informs the final building. Allusions to fellow architects in his own work are oblique, parodic, or understated; many throb softly just below the threshold of recognition. Just as the ground plan of MIT's Stata Center recalls the compacted plans of Giambattista Piranesi and John Soane, the great

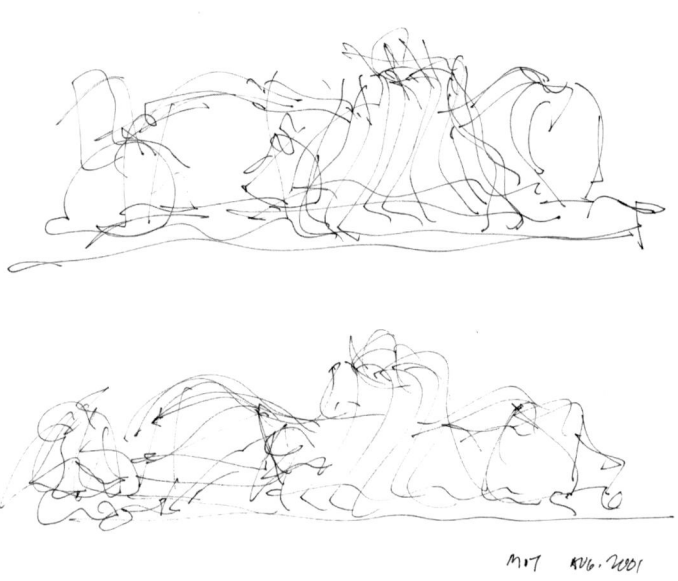

Figure 41. Jerusalem Museum of Tolerance — Center for Human Dignity, a Project of the Simon Wiesenthal Center, Jerusalem, Israel, 2001

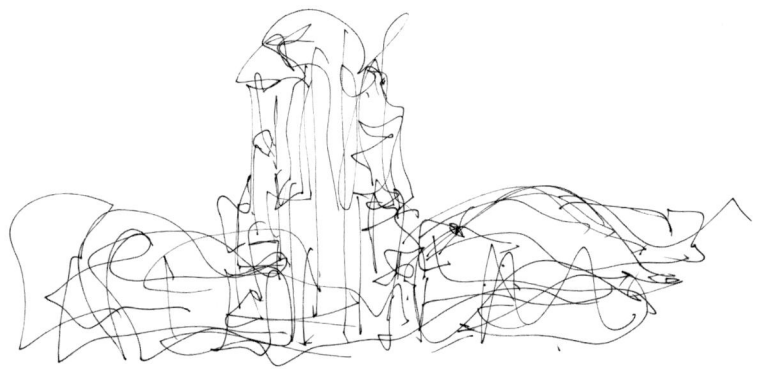

PRINCETON AUG. '02

Figure 42. The Peter B. Lewis Science Library, Princeton University, Princeton, New Jersey, 2002

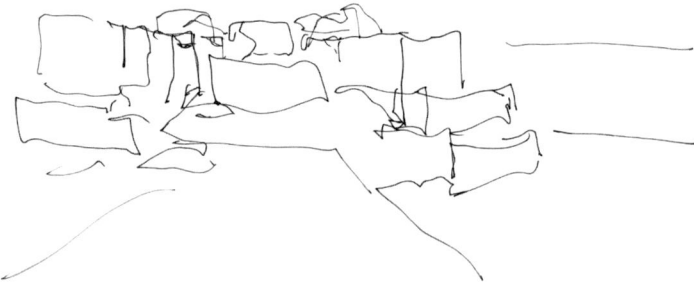

Figure 43. University of Toledo Center for the Visual Arts, Toledo, Ohio, 1990

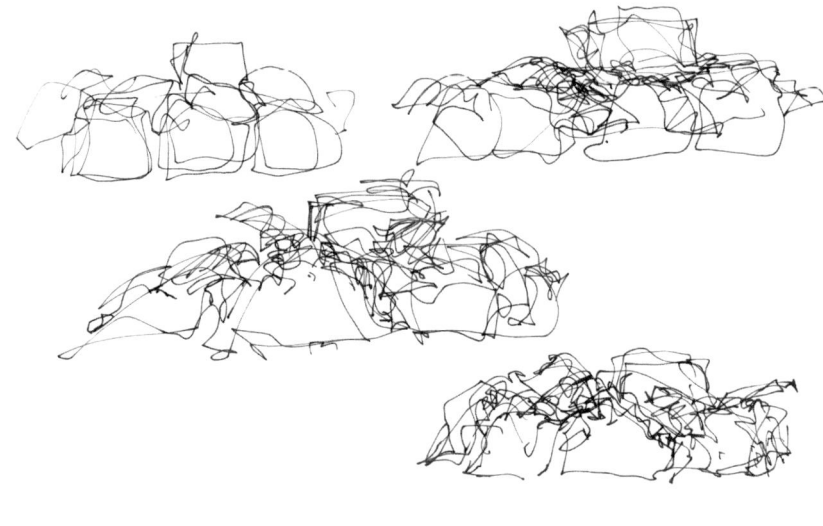

Figure 44. Experience Music Project, Seattle, Washington, undated

billowing folds in the Walt Disney Concert Hall or the Museum of Tolerance faintly echo Francesco Borromini's exuberant and unconventional syntax, with its continuous curves and countercurves (see figs. 33 and 41). Direct quotations are rare. In Princeton University's Science Library, a secular version of the old learned monastery, a cutout on the floor quotes playfully from Baroque architecture: "'we have looked at Borromini a lot. Particularly San Carlo. The elliptical shape of the interior is a very dynamic form,'" comments Craig Webb, adding that they also looked closely at the architecture of Guarino Guarini, another bold Baroque iconoclast.[54] The reference, deliberately deformed and visible only in the plan, is difficult to read (figs. 45–46). Direct citations are seldom reflected in Gehry's sketches, where such explicit details would threaten spontaneity and slow down the hurried pace of speculation.

Less obvious, but more important is the influence of the great masters of twentieth-century architecture that reverberates in all of Gehry's built works. Here, too, the sketches give scarcely a hint of Le Corbusier, whose late work Gehry studied so carefully, or of Aalto, though the warm wooden interiors of the Walt Disney Concert Hall pay homage to the humane legacy of the Finnish

master. Japanese architecture, a major influence on
Gehry's work thanks to its sensitive scale and natural
materials and textures, also had no impact on the
sketches. Perhaps one of his strongest affinities in this
respect lies with the German Expressionists—Hans
Poelzig, Hans Scharoun, or Bruno Taut, great draftsmen
all—not only in the pent-up energy of some of Gehry's
sketches (see fig. 44) but also in his conception of the art
of building. "'Architecture is art,'" wrote Taut, "'and ought
to be the highest of the arts. It consists exclusively of
powerful emotion and addresses itself exclusively to the
emotions.'"[55] The affinities are hardly fortuitous. LACMA
commissioned Gehry to design its exhibition of German
Expressionist sculpture in 1983, and to this day Germany
remains the country in which Gehry has built the most
outside the United States.

Gehry's sources are varied, deep, and un-literal: "There
is a misconception about my work—that I just make
shapes and there is no inside. I don't know how people
see or get that idea. It looks like we're tearing up paper
to make models, and I just roll up the paper and throw it
all out. It's not like that. It is much more precise and
careful. We work from the inside out, mostly. What's
more, as someone very involved with sculpture and art

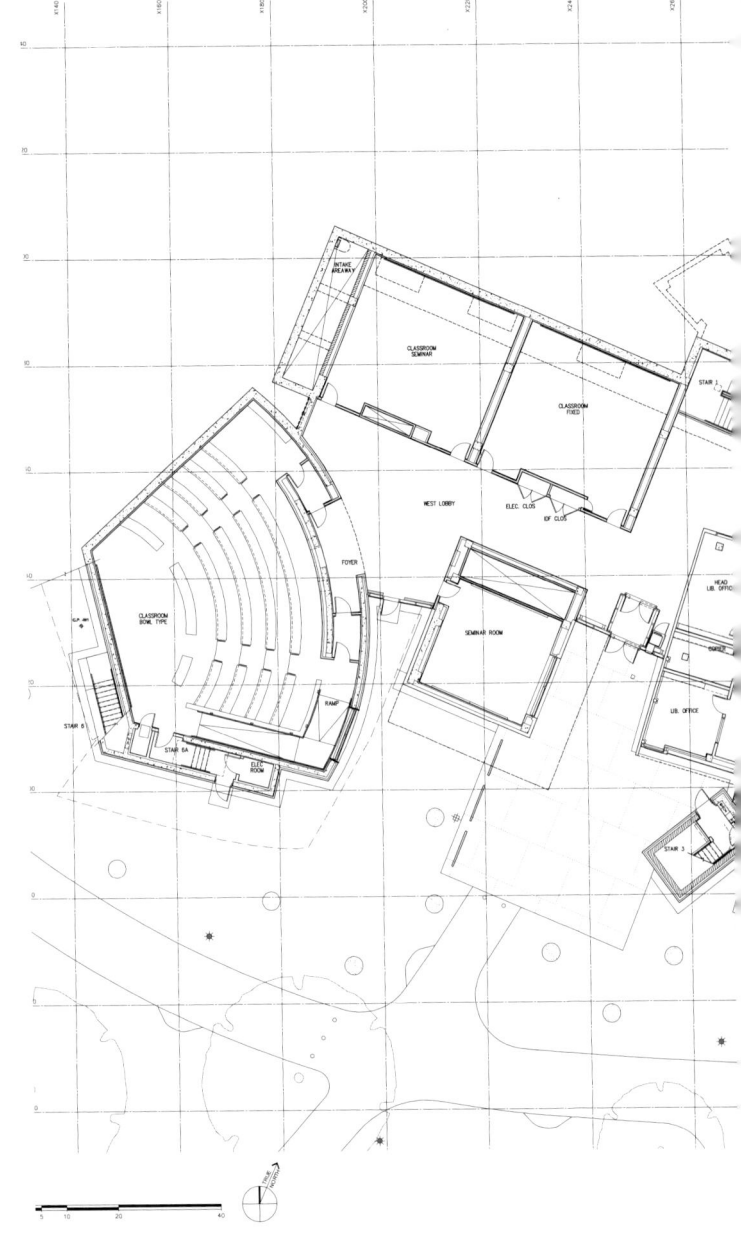

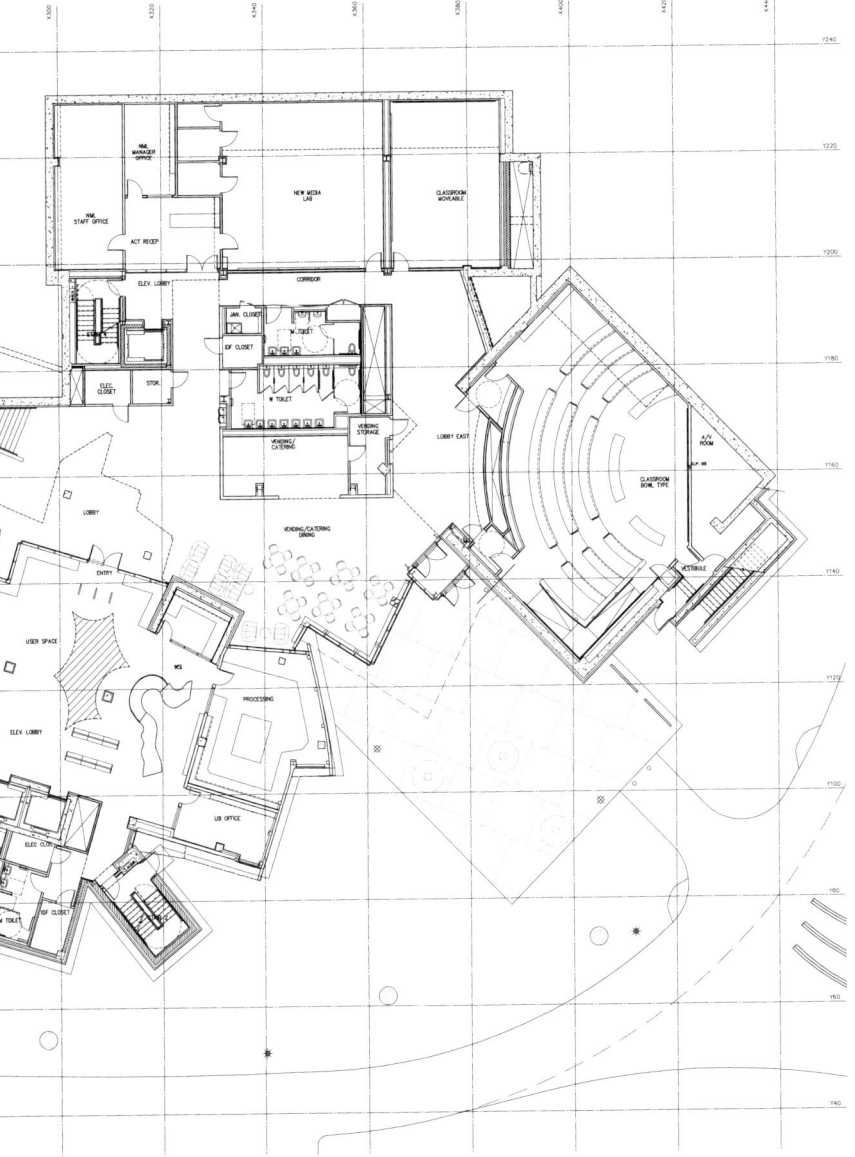

Figure 45. The Peter B. Lewis Science Library, Princeton University, Princeton, New Jersey, first floor plan, 2008

and dance and music—those things are part of my life—I
take my nourishment from them."[56] An avid concertgoer,
Gehry has been closely associated with composers,
musicians, and conductors active in Los Angeles, like
John Adams, Pierre Boulez, and Esa-Pekka Salonen.
Gehry's interest in music dates back to his undergraduate
days when he performed in a Gagaku orchestra at the
University of Southern California.[57] For the inauguration
of the Temporary Contemporary in Los Angeles, in 1983,
he designed sets for *Available Light*, with choreography
by Lucinda Childs and music by John Adams. When
Gehry's Richard B. Fisher Center for the Performing Arts
opened to the public at Bard College in Annadale-on-
Hudson, New York, in 2003, he created set designs for
Leoš Janáček's opera *Osud*. From art and music to
visual urban culture and its messy, sprawling idioms, the
Canadian-born Gehry has understood the American
landscape as few natives have. Like Charles Ives, he
embraces—and transcends—innumerable aspects of
what is thoroughly American, high or low, high *and* low.

In Conclusion

Frank Gehry clearly loves to draw. His sketches, like his
architecture, seem to imply a deep-seated revolt against
the suppression of the notion of pleasure in Modernist

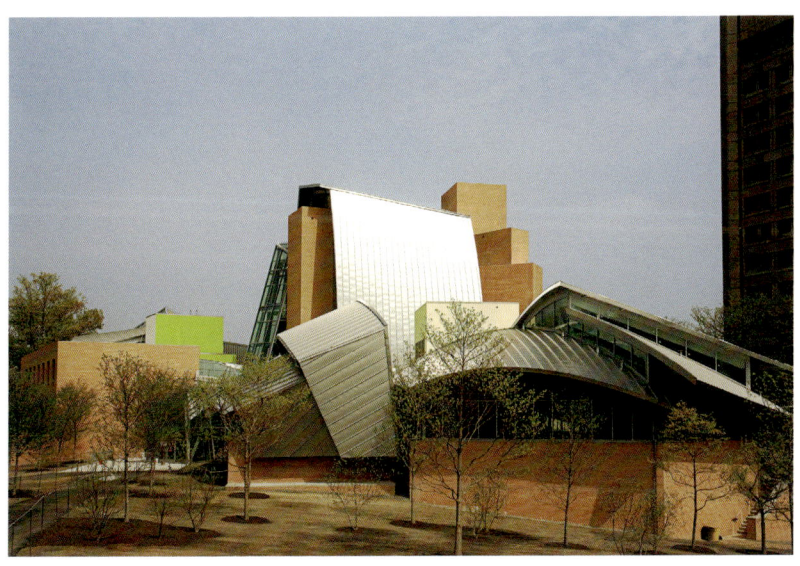

Figure 46. The Peter B. Lewis Science Library, Princeton University, Princeton, New Jersey, 2008

architecture. Sometimes he gets carried away as he extemporizes, elated by the driving force of the drawing, aestheticizing the slips of the pen, the inadvertent strokes and loops that come with sketching swiftly. Some of these unpremeditated forms will pass into the final work, regardless of program and budget. The architect Michael Graves, himself a master in this area, has neatly captured the determining role of draftsmanship: "If we are ultimately discussing the quality of architecture which results from a mode of conceptualization, then certainly the level of richness is increased by the component of inquiry derived from the art of drawing itself."[58]

By subjecting these drawings to rigorous selection and exhibiting them in public, museums intervene in their meanings and insert them in an overarching narrative in which they appear effortless and hardly suggest the long years of apprenticeship or the process of trial and error that culminates in the finely calibrated sketch. Museum settings suggest that drawings should be judged on their own intrinsic merits, and not merely as signifiers for architectural referents. As a means of self-expression, sketches convey the architect's personal vision; but they also exceed intentionality, and carry their own truths and associations. The very best communicate something more, the ability of art to speak from a higher vantage point: "'I equally recognize that the notable works in any and every medium have always existed on many other levels,'" Gehry stated. "'It is these levels beyond function that not only allow architecture to maximize its possibilities, but also allow a society to use architecture as one of the means by which it expresses individual and collective consciousness.'"[59] In their unfettered freedom, sketches offer a glimpse of the imagination at work in that luminous, half-palpable realm where the vanishing thought leaves traces in its wake: the stuff of dreams.

I would like to express my gratitude to Charlotte Hyde, who sent me crucial material from Los Angeles; Rosemarie Haag Bletter, Mary McLeod, and Carol McMichael Reese for their thoughtful reading of the manuscript and numerous suggestions; and John Pinto for his advice on the history of architectural drawings. I also wish to thank my toughest critic, my husband, Christopher Hailey.

1 Terence Riley, "Drawn into a Collection: A Context of Practices," in *Envisioning Architecture: Drawings from the Museum of Modern Art*, ed. Matilda McQuaid, exh. cat., Museum of Modern Art (New York, 2002), 11.

2 John Whiteman, "Criticism, Representation and Experience in Contemporary Architecture: Architecture and Drawing in an Age of Criticism," *Harvard Architecture Review* 6 (1987): 144.

3 Gehry, Peter Eisenman, and Thom Mayne, among others, have spoken freely of their experience with psychoanalysis. The late Milton Wexler, whom Gehry saw for thirty-five years, was even interviewed in Sydney Pollack's film *Sketches of Frank Gehry* (2006).

4 Daniel M. Herbert, "Study Drawings in Architectural Design: Their Properties as a Graphic Medium," *Journal of Architectural Education* 41, no. 2 (Winter 1988): 26–27.

5 Frank Lloyd Wright, "In the Cause of Architecture. 1. The Logic of the Plan," *Architectural Record* 63, no. 1 (January 1928): 49.

6 Frank Gehry, interview with the author, August 28, 2006, Los Angeles.

7 "No, I'm an Architect': Frank Gehry and Peter Arnell: A Conversation," in *Frank Gehry: Buildings and Projects*, ed. Peter Arnell and Ted Bickford (New York: Rizzoli, 1985), xv.

8 Alberto Pérez-Gómez and Louise Pelletier, "Architectural Representation beyond Perspectivism," *Perspecta* 27 (1992): 21.

9 Gehry interview, August 28, 2006.

10 Stanislaus von Moos, "Le Corbusier as Painter," *Oppositions* 19–20 (Winter/Spring 1980): 95.

11 "But that was the tradition for architects to do travel sketches, but I never got into that. I never got into that. I don't draw like that. I can draw like that but I don't like the drawing. I don't like those drawings. I don't like travel sketches. . . . It's just a preference. I think part of the reason that I don't is that when I came out of architecture school, I went to Europe, saw all the stuff, came back, went to work, I worked for Victor Gruen's office. I worked for Carlos Diniz. I did renderings. In the army and after the army, I did renderings and I needed it. I did it for a living. I think it was that experience— blocking out perspectives mechanically, endlessly." Gehry interview, August 28, 2006.

12 Mark Rappolt and Robert Violette, "Editor's Note," in *Gehry Draws*, ed. Mark Rappolt and Robert Violette (Cambridge, Mass.: MIT Press, 2004), 8.

13 Robin Evans, "Architectural Projection," in *Architecture and Its Image: Four Centuries of Architectural Representation*, ed. Eve Blau and Edward Kaufman (Montreal: Canadian Centre for Architecture, 1989), 20.

14 Pollack quoted in Mary McNamara, "From One Artist to Another," *Los Angeles Times*, May 14, 2006, E32.

15 Evans, "Architectural Projection," 21.

16 In Arnell and Bickford, eds., *Frank Gehry*, xv.

17 Robert Ivy, "Frank Gehry: Plain Talk with a Master," *Architectural Record* 187, no. 5 (May 1999): 189.

18 Herbert, "Study Drawings," 32.

19 Werner Oechslin, "The Well-Tempered Sketch," *Daidalos* 5 (September 1982): 99.

20 Paul Valéry, *Degas Danse Dessin* (Paris: Gallimard, 1938), 25.

21 Evans, "Architectural Projection," 33–34.

22 In Rappolt and Violette, eds., *Gehry Draws*, 392.

23 Roland Barthes, *Camera Lucida: Reflections on Photography*, trans. Richard Howard (New York: Hill and Wang, 1981), 6.

24 Germano Celant, "Reflections on Frank Gehry," in *Frank Gehry*, ed. Arnell and Bickford, 11. For Francesco Dal Co, visitors to Gehry's buildings are confronted "by sensations of disorientation caused by vast, directionless spaces, like three-dimensional expansions of his sketches, lines entangled like balls of yarn (and this is why we cannot help but view Gehry's sketches as the expressions of a sort of 'automatic writing')." See "The World Turned Upside-Down: The Tortoise Flies and the Hare Threatens the Lion," in Francesco Dal Co and Kurt W. Forster, *Frank O. Gehry: The Complete Works* (Milan: Electa, 2005), 55.

25 Gehry interview, August 28, 2006.

26 Juhani Pallasmaa, *The Eyes of the Skin: Architecture and the Senses* (Chichester, England: John Wiley and Sons, 2005), 42.

27 W. B. Yeats, "Among School Children," in *The Collected Poems of W. B. Yeats* (New York: Macmillan, 1956), 214.

28 Gehry quoted in Beatriz Colomina, "The House that Built Gehry," in *Frank Gehry, Architect*, ed. J. Fiona Ragheb, exh. cat., Solomon R. Guggenheim Museum (New York, 2001), 308.

29 Alan Riding, "Vuitton Plans a Gehry-Designed Arts Center in Paris," *New York Times*, October 3, 2006, E3.

30 Michael Sorkin, "Frozen Light," in *Gehry Talks: Architecture + Process*, ed. Mildred Friedman, rev. ed. (New York: Universe Publishing, 2002), 30. Gehry himself does not use the computer, but his aides rely on it to transform his ideas and sketches into exact documents for contractors.

31 Gehry quoted in Carol Burns, "The Gehry Phenomenon," in *Thinking the Present: Recent American Architecture*, ed. K. Michael Hays and Carol Burns (New York: Princeton Architectural Press, 1990), 82–83.

32 Barbaralee Diamonstein, "Frank O. Gehry," in *American Architecture Now*, ed. Barbaralee Diamonstein (New York: Rizzoli, 1980), 37.

33 Mark A. Hewitt, "The Imaginary Mountain: The Significance of Contour in Alvar Aalto's Sketches," *Perspecta* 25 (1989): 164.

34 I wish to thank Carol McMichael Reese for having called my attention to the use of cameras inside Gehry's models.

35 Frank Gehry, "Commentaries," in *Gehry Talks*, ed. Friedman, 47–48.

36 Gehry quoted in Mildred Friedman, "Architecture in Motion," in *Frank Gehry, Architect*, ed. Ragheb, 296.

37 Webb quoted in *Gehry Draws*, ed. Rappolt and Violette, 126.

38 Gehry quoted in Beatriz Colomina, "A Conversation with Frank Gehry," *El Croquis* 117 (2003): 14.

39 Gehry quoted in Janet Nairn, "Frank Gehry: The Search for a 'No Rules' Architecture," *Architectural Record* 159, no. 6 (June 1976): 95.

40 The give-and-take was mutual. To produce his torqued pieces, Serra has on occasion appealed to Gehry's engineers for help with CATIA. See David Sylvester, "Interview," in *Richard Serra: Sculpture, 1985–1998*, exh. cat., Museum of Contemporary Art (Los Angeles, 1998), 188.

41 "Architecture has been a great encyclopedia of thought for me," notes Serra. "Not that I want to make architecture, but it has enabled me to understand space in relation to movement. That cannot be learned from the histories of representation and object-making in sculpture." Quoted in Kynaston McShine, "A Conversation about Work with Richard Serra," in *Richard Serra Sculpture: Forty Years*, ed. Kynaston McShine and Lynne Cooke (New York: Museum of Modern Art, 2007), 32.

42 Ivy, "Frank Gehry: Plain Talk," 190.

43 Esther McCoy, "What You Know, You Question," *Progressive Architecture* 67, no. 10 (October 1986): 75.

44 His show was called *A New View: The Architect's Eye*. See Dal Co and Forster, *Frank O. Gehry*, 460.

45 Cristina Bechtler, ed., *Frank O. Gehry, Kurt W. Forster* (Ostfildern-Ruit: Cantz, 1999), 53.

46 Frank Gehry, interview with John Tusa, BBC Radio 3. Accessed online at http://www.bbc.co.uk/radio3/johntusainterview/gehry_transcript.shtml.

47 Walter Benjamin, "The Work of Art in the Age of Mechanical Reproduction," in *Illuminations*, ed. and with an introduction by Hannah Arendt (New York: Schocken, 1977), 239.

48 Gehry interview, August 28, 2006.

49 For the problems involved, see Harrison Fraker, "Spatial and Material Conventions: Frank Gehry's Artistic References," in *Midgård* 1, no. 1 (1987): 105–15. See also Gavin Macrae-Gibson, *The Secret Life of Buildings: An American Mythology for Modern Architecture* (Cambridge, Mass.: MIT Press, 1985), 2–29.

50 Friedman, ed., *Gehry Talks*, 42.

51 Webb quoted in *Gehry Draws*, ed. Rappolt and Violette, 190. For Morandi, see "Conversation between Frank O. Gehry and Kurt W. Forster with Cristina Bechtler," in *Frank O. Gehry, Kurt W. Forster*, ed. Bechtler, 31.

52 See Flavio Fergonzi, "Catalog of Works," in *The Later Morandi*, ed. Laura Mattioli Rossi (Milan: Mazzotta, 1998), 104.

53 Riding, "Vuitton Plans a Gehry-Designed Arts Center." The idea was unusual but not unprecedented; in 2002 Elizabeth Diller and Ricardo Scofidio designed the Blur Building, in Switzerland, another manufactured cloud.

54 Craig Webb, personal communication to the author, October 12, 2007. Serra also claimed to have derived inspiration for one of his pieces, *Torqued Ellipse IV* (1998) from Borromini's San Carlo. See McShine, "A Conversation," 33.

55 Taut quoted in Wolfgang Pehnt, *Expressionist Architecture* (New York: Praeger, 1973), 20. The auditorium at the Walt Disney Concert Hall can trace its lineage back to Scharoun's Philharmonie in Berlin, as can the ground plan of MIT's Stata Center, which has other sources as well.

56 In Rappolt and Violette, eds., *Gehry Draws*, 234.

57 On October 12, 2004, on the occasion of a presentation of the Gagaku ensemble of the Japanese Imperial Court, Gehry gave a preconcert lecture in the Walt Disney Concert Hall in the company of his former teacher from USC, Robert Garfias, who is a specialist on the Gagaku.

58 Michael Graves, "The Necessity for Drawing: Tangible Speculation," *Architectural Design* 47, no. 6 (1977): 393–94.

59 Gehry quoted in "Frank O. Gehry," in *The California Condition: A Pregnant Architecture*, exh. cat., La Jolla Museum of Contemporary Art (La Jolla, Calif., 1982), 40.

Selected Bibliography

Adams, Brooks. "Frank Gehry's Merzbau."
Art in America 76, no. 11 (November 1988):
139–44, 205.

The Architecture of Frank Gehry. Exh. cat.,
Walker Art Center. Minneapolis, 1986.

Arnell, Peter, and Ted Bickford, eds. *Frank
Gehry: Buildings and Projects.* New York:
Rizzoli, 1985.

Bechtler, Cristina, ed. *Frank O. Gehry, Kurt W.
Forster.* Ostfildern-Ruit: Cantz, 1999.

Burns, Carol. "The Gehry Phenomenon." In
*Thinking the Present: Recent American
Architecture*, edited by K. Michael Hays and
Carol Burns, 72–88. New York: Princeton
Architectural Press, 1990.

*The California Condition: A Pregnant
Architecture.* Exh. cat., La Jolla Museum of
Contemporary Art. La Jolla, Calif., 1982.

Dal Co, Francesco, and Kurt W. Forster.
Frank O. Gehry: The Complete Works. Milan:
Electa, 2005.

Diamonstein, Barbaralee. "Frank O. Gehry."
In *American Architecture Now*, edited by
Barbaralee Diamonstein, 34–46. New York:
Rizzoli, 1980.

Evans, Robin. "Architectural Projection." In
*Architecture and Its Image: Four Centuries of

Architectural Representation*, edited by Eve
Blau and Edward Kaufman, 19–35. Montreal:
Canadian Centre for Architecture, 1989.

FOG: Flowing in All Directions. Exh. cat.,
Museum of Contemporary Art. Los Angeles,
2003.

Fraker, Harrison. "Spatial and Material
Conventions: Frank Gehry's Artistic
References." *Midgård* 1, no. 1 (1987): 105–15.

"Frank Gehry from A to Z." Special issue,
El Croquis, no. 117 (2003).

Friedman, Mildred, ed. *Gehry Talks:
Architecture + Process.* Rev. ed. New York:
Universe Publishing, 2002.

Graves, Michael. "The Necessity for Drawing:
Tangible Speculation." *Architectural Design* 47,
no. 6 (1977): 384–94

Herbert, Daniel M. "Study Drawings in
Architectural Design: Their Properties as a
Graphic Medium." *Journal of Architectural
Education* 41, no. 2 (Winter 1988): 26–38.

Hewitt, Mark A. "Representational Forms and
Modes of Conception: An Approach to the
History of Architectural Drawing." *Journal of
Architectural Education* 39, no. 2 (Winter
1985): 2–9.

Ivy, Robert. "Frank Gehry: Plain Talk with a
Master." *Architectural Record* 187, no. 5
(May 1999): 184–92, 356, 359–60.

Lacy, Bill. "Interview with FOG." In *Angels and Franciscans: Innovative Architecture from Los Angeles and San Francisco,* edited by Bill Lacy and Susan de Menil, 8–16. New York: Rizzoli, 1992.

Leclerc, David. "Frank Gehry, un moment de vérité." *L'Architecture d'aujourd'hui,* no. 286 (April 1993): 78–91.

Macrae-Gibson, Gavin. *The Secret Life of Buildings: An American Mythology for Modern Architecture.* Cambridge, Mass.: MIT Press, 1985.

McCoy, Esther. "What You Know, You Question." *Progressive Architecture* 67, no. 10 (October 1986): 75.

McQuaid, Matilda, ed. *Envisioning Architecture: Drawings from the Museum of Modern Art.* Exh. cat., Museum of Modern Art. New York, 2002.

Nairn, Janet. "Frank Gehry: The Search for a 'No Rules' Architecture." *Architectural Record* 159, no. 6 (June 1976): 95–102.

Oechslin, Werner. "The Well-Tempered Sketch." *Daidalos* 5 (September 1982): 99–112.

Pérez-Gómez, Alberto, and Louise Pelletier. "Architectural Representation beyond Perspectivism." *Perspecta* 27 (1992): 21–39.

Ragheb, J. Fiona, ed. *Frank Gehry, Architect.* Exh. cat., Solomon R. Guggenheim Museum. New York, 2001.

Rappolt, Mark, and Robert Violette, eds. *Gehry Draws.* Cambridge, Mass.: MIT Press, 2004.

Reese, Carol McMichael. "Frank Gehry in Conversation with Ernest Fleischmann." In *Late Thoughts: Reflections on Artists and Composers at Work,* edited by Karen Painter and Thomas Crow, 97–113. Los Angeles: Getty Research Institute, 2006.

Whiteman, John. "Criticism, Representation and Experience in Contemporary Architecture: Architecture and Drawing in an Age of Criticism." *Harvard Architecture Review* 6 (1987): 137–47.

Zardini, Mirko, ed. *Frank O. Gehry: America as Context.* Milan: Electa, 1994.

Photography Credits